Countering Violent Extremism

Countering Violent Extremism

The International Deradicalization Agenda

Tahir Abbas

I.B. TAURIS
LONDON • NEW YORK • OXFORD • NEW DELHI • SYDNEY

I.B. TAURIS
Bloomsbury Publishing Plc
50 Bedford Square, London, WC1B 3DP, UK
1385 Broadway, New York, NY 10018, USA
29 Earlsfort Terrace, Dublin 2, Ireland

BLOOMSBURY, I.B. TAURIS and the I.B. Tauris logo
are trademarks of Bloomsbury Publishing Plc

First published in Great Britain 2021

Copyright © Tahir Abbas, 2021

Tahir Abbas has asserted his right under the Copyright, Designs
and Patents Act, 1988, to be identified as Author of this work.

For legal purposes the Acknowledgements on p. x constitute
an extension of this copyright page.

Cover design by Holly Bell

All rights reserved. No part of this publication may be reproduced or transmitted in any form or by any means, electronic or mechanical, including photocopying, recording, or any information storage or retrieval system, without prior permission in writing from the publishers.

Bloomsbury Publishing Plc does not have any control over, or responsibility for, any third-party websites referred to or in this book. All internet addresses given in this book were correct at the time of going to press. The author and publisher regret any inconvenience caused if addresses have changed or sites have ceased to exist, but can accept no responsibility for any such changes.

A catalogue record for this book is available from the British Library.

A catalog record for this book is available from the Library of Congress

ISBN:	HB:	978-1-8386-0722-7
	PB:	978-1-7883-1069-7
	ePDF:	978-1-8386-0724-1
	eBook:	978-1-8386-0723-4

Typeset by Integra Software Services Pvt Ltd.,

To find out more about our authors and books visit www.bloomsbury.com
and sign up for our newsletters.

For Toby Zayn

Contents

About the book   viii
Acknowledgements   x

Part One   Terrorism and states
1   Definitional challenges   3
2   State terrorism   17
3   The counter-terror state   29
4   Genocide and ethnic cleansing   39

Part Two   Disentangling violent extremism
5   Individual factors in terrorism   53
6   The social science of extremism   67
7   Reciprocal radicalization   79
8   Countering reciprocal radicalization   93
9   The UK 'Prevent' agenda   105

Part Three   Deradicalization
10   Leaving terrorism behind   119
11   Disordered deradicalization   133
12   Driven to hate   149
13   Terror politics   161

Notes   175
Bibliography   195
Index   210

About the book

In attempting to understand the concept of countering violent extremism (CVE), not only is it a paradigm with roots in policies of deradicalization, prevention, disengagement and counter-extremism, it is also fraught with tension, inconsistencies and huge polarizations.

This book aims to assesses the nature of the overarching approach of the concept, but also explore how terrorism and radicalization have become particular sociological, political and cultural concerns, examining matters in local, national and global contexts. In various attempts to understand the issues from different standpoints, countering extremism paradigms have the potential to divide individuals and institutions in considerable ways. In reality, CVE projects are widely experienced not as attempts to necessarily deal with the issues that cause radicalization and terrorism in a specific or a general sense. In reality, CVE initiatives that have a real-world application often deliver community and youth development projects as a process of social engineering. They aim to discourage, disengage and dis-incentivize vulnerable young people on the verge of radical political views that could lead to violence. However, without alleviating structural inequality or issues arising from problematic (re)integration policy, which are important considerations in motivating would-be extremisms of various kinds, the results are likely to remain limited.

The growing problem of far-right extremism is emerging reciprocally to Islamism. Extremism and violence do not emerge in a vacuum – nor do the policies that counter these concerns. The role of governments and issues relating to 'state terrorism' and the 'counter-terror state' are further important considerations. However, given the historically dominant focus on violent Islamism over other types of terrorism, there are ongoing concerns relating to a postcolonial framework concerning the focus on Muslim groups, at home and abroad. The problems of violent extremism (VE) are local and so are therefore the solutions, while the questions of state terror relate more to growing instances of ethnic or religious nationalism sweeping much of the world at present. This book argues that to alleviate the patterns of violence that create concerns for societies across the world, North and South, issues of radicalization and terrorism – which relate directly to politics and matters of social cohesion – require bottom-up, community-driven and wholly inclusive interventions.

Acknowledgements

I am grateful to Olivia Dellow for her kind assistance in the eventual production of the book with Bloomsbury Academic, which started life when I first began thinking about the concept at the Royal United Services Institute in London. I am also extremely grateful to Mohammed S. Elshimi for the candid conversations on the topic and for sharing his deep insights with me. The book was completed at the Institute of Security and Global Affairs of Leiden University in The Hague where I now teach around the topics more generally while continuing to pursue my research interests in ethnicity, radicalization, Islamophobia and terrorism. I am grateful to my erudite colleagues for sharing their wisdom and insights with me, in particular, my enthusiastic, supportive and astute fellow scholars from the Terrorism and Political Violence Group. I am also thankful to my students taking my various courses on the Crisis and Security Management Masters programme. Their intelligent questions, genuine concerns over the state of the world and their ambitions to make a difference have been inspiring.

During the time it took to write this book, I had the privilege of travelling to numerous countries and cities to discuss the dynamics of CVE and its delivery. I am grateful for the opportunity to give invited to talks and presentations at Queen's University in Kingston and Public Safety in Ottawa, Canada; United States Institute of Peace in Washington DC; St. John's College, Cambridge University; University of Aberdeen; Manchester Metropolitan University; King's College London; Portcullis House and House of Commons, Westminster; Security and Counter Terror Expo at the London Olympia; Lancaster University; European Policy Centre in Brussels; Federal Agency for Civic Education in Potsdam; Ljubljana University; National University of Science and Technology in Islamabad, as well as opportunities to take part in panels or chair them in Marrakesh, Addis Ababa and Jakarta.

Part One

Terrorism and states

1

Definitional challenges

An introduction to the book

The study of terrorism, questions of radicalization and the value of deradicalization interventions have preoccupied social scientists, policymakers and community groups for a considerable period. However, the events of 9/11, the 'war on terror', the growth of European jihadis and the rise and fall of Islamic State in Iraq and Syria, and questions concerning the return of foreign fighters, have created new challenges without clear answers. This book is an attempt to survey the complexities of these topics by providing a detailed account of the issues that reveal the problems of extremism, radicalization and terrorism on the one hand and the role of states, either through state terrorism or as the counter-terror state, to help eradicate the problems or potentially worsen them, on the other.

Even though terrorism is a social construction and difficulties often arise in establishing the facts, including the psychological and sociological makeup of assailants, there is also the question of who defines the problem. The adage that 'one man's terrorist is another man's freedom fighter' has remained consistent throughout history. Terrorizing people in societies has long been associated with individuals and groups who have particular ideological or political objectives, where the act itself is the message that these groups wish to convey. To terrify ordinary members of the public is to target innocent civilians in the hope of obtaining a response from state actors who often insist 'we will not negotiate with terrorists' but in reality, behind the scenes, deals are made, prisoners are exchanged and negotiations are held. History continues to demonstrate the only real way of solving terrorism carried out by various groups is to incorporate them into the political process (or to eliminate them). These notions are important in any analysis of terrorism and violent extremism (VE), but it is also clear that the nature of terrorism has changed in the light of the 'war on terror' and, in particular, the role of the online space in recruitment, preparation and activation of terrorists – who evolve, learn and adapt to different opportunity structures. It is imperative to ask critical questions; especially in cases where states are the perpetrators of violent acts which cause terror among the population but receive scant attention. The idea that 'new terrorism' is different from the old – that is, religious zeal is the dominating motive – is a somewhat of a distraction from the reality that myriad motivations exist among violent extremist groups, and though religion is often as the veneer, the context is always political. Kashmir and Palestine are two territories that have faced terrorism carried out by states – both strategic and structural – but the general attention on non-state actors takes attention away from genuine freedom struggles. Radicalization is a contested concept yet there is an assumption that what it means is clear. It grants a licence to states to produce counter-terrorism (CT) and CVE policy in whatever form selected.

The 'war on terror' was a response to terror, but it has produced further terror, which currently remains in perpetuity. It has created more havoc in the Muslim world, and more attacks on the West. New forms of state terrorism include the use of drones as racist biopolitics – one that is deliberate – and faceless. It is impossible to ignore the importance of understanding genocide and ethnic cleansing as types of state terrorism against non-combatants. Both have significant implications. In recent periods, with examples in Kashmir, Myanmar and former Yugoslavia adding new perspectives on the idea of 'ethnic cleansing of Muslims', ongoing concerns in Xinjiang in eastern China are further cause for concern. Terrorist activity is essentially situational, but too much of CVE policy focuses on the ideological 'pull factors' while rendering the 'push factors' (namely structural, institutional and political) almost invisible. To help better understand these concerns, research and policy should incorporate criminology, psychology, sociology and international relations concepts into the analysis to avoid the consequences of costly errors. In this milieu, recognizing personal grievances are essential. For example, Salafism does not always have to lead to violence – nor does Islamism per se.[1] It is violent jihadism that is the most significant issue in the final analysis. In this regard, a deeper understanding of the social-psychological dimension that focuses on an individual's relationships with space and place is also a critical factor. Marginalized economic relations facing both Muslim minorities in Western Europe and indigenous white groups are also associated with the decline of historical conceptions of masculinity. With notions of diversity problematized in many settings, it is compounded by a 'war on terror culture' that overlooks social mobility, integration and questions of citizenship and belonging – for all.

Reciprocal radicalization is a growing problem throughout Europe. Here, national politics is fundamental, with populism, authoritarianism and majoritarian nationalism becoming significant concerns as mainstream media drives the sentiments that politicians repackage in an unholy alliance. However, to counter reciprocal radicalization is to strengthen the resolve communities through education and online awareness, although they have yet to be fully tested in practice. What works, in reality, is largely dependent on national political culture as well as regional and domestic policy frameworks. But there are so many unanswered questions – and only some indication of success; however, what is clear is that it is important to see these as nuanced terms – and opportunities, where tailor-made approaches are to be applied, which, apart from some country cases, make it extremely difficult to make any generalizations. Socio-economic divisions are exacerbated by populist authoritarianism and hate towards others, in particular, feeding off and into the insecurities facing men. Former President Trump of the United States and Prime Minister Boris Johnson of the United Kingdom are two obvious examples, but both are the symptom – not the cause – of the malaise.

Foreign fighters are not new. They have existed since the dawn of the modern era, yet dominant theories concerning Islamist extremism that focus on transnationalism are weak. The idea of centralized Islamism as the single most important driving force is also inadequate. The fact that one in three of the approximately 300 Dutch jihadis who travelled to Iraq and Syria to join the Islamic State were indigenous white men and women who converted should provide a perspective that suggests that these jihadis, men and women, minorities and majorities, are 'made' in their countries of birth. In reality, radicalization today is occurring online but it is not always clear how. The processes of radicalization are much more about politics and society than vulnerable individuals who are susceptible to external influences. The concept of CVE will remain in the spotlight – but the evidence base needs to improve – and important questions need to be asked of states as well as vulnerable individuals from all backgrounds, not just the Islamists.

The study of terrorism, VE, and the nature of ethnic, social and religious conflict are of primary concern in a world riven with division and discord. How issues are understood and responded to, however, reflect more on the motivations of policymakers whose aims vary depending on questions of resources, time and the political climate. The understanding of terrorism and CT is often skewed due to various institutional effects, which has a bearing on policy at one level but also the resultant effect of community relations at another level. For example, in the context of radical Islamism as well as far-right extremism both sets of opposing groups are motivated by Islamophobia that feeds off aspects of an anti-Muslim discourse, which has implications for radicalization, including recruitment.[2]

But before it is possible to explore the complexity of these issues, it is necessary to address some definitional challenges. A significant dimension to understanding terrorism is the study of central topics within the social sciences that relate to questions of terrorism. These include questions of power, authority and discourse. There are also questions regarding identity, social change and the impact of economic transformation. There are local issues to consider but in the realms of neoliberal globalization, what happens in other parts of the world can have a direct bearing on what occurs in various local area settings. However, terrorism, political violence and the discourse surrounding these concepts have meaning only in social context, and the lens through which any single individual views their experiences. Violent extremism and terrorism could be argued to be a function of society – as much as it is a reality of extremist groups or individuals who engage in violence due to ideological motivations. If so, how do these issues play out in reality and how can we take our 'knowledge' and introduce interventions that yield positive impact?

The media is a significant cause of the mixed message on what terrorism is.[3] Terrorism itself is aimed at attracting media attention, which either helps or supports the aims of those wanting to carry out the terrorist acts in the first instance – namely to spread a political or ideological message through an act of violence or threat of violence, usually targeted at innocent civilians or specific state institutions. In almost all cases, '[v]irtually any especially abhorrent act of violence perceived as directed against society – whether it involves the activities of anti-government dissidents or governments themselves, organized-crime syndicates, common criminals, rioting mobs, people engaged in militant protest, individual psychotics, or lone extortionists – is often labelled "terrorism".[4] From this, it can be stated that terrorism is, at least, a political question, which suggests it has political aims. These aims include changing the nature of society in a violently radical way, which is presented as another form of social change, albeit more aggressively. It suggests that terrorism is related to questioning power; namely challenging the instruments in society that wield power, raising to the fore questions on the nature of this power and its implications.

Therefore, power is at the heart of terrorism because power is also a fundamental concept in society, where complex human relations are intertwined with multiple meanings, outcomes and problems that all rest on power, including its access or the problems caused by its inequitable distribution. In such cases, terrorism, therefore, can be a 'planned, calculated, and indeed systematic act'.[5] In reaching this understanding when trying to comprehend what terrorism is, the question remains as to why a degree of confusion persists. The answer is that the meaning has changed over time.

The historical dimension

Given the preponderance of modern definitions that mandate that terrorism is against the state, the concept was first used to describe the actions of the state. Originally used during the French Revolution, the idea of state terror was a means by which the state could control or manage the growing problems of what was at the time a form of violence and extremism that emerged during a period of major social and political instability. This rule, known as the *reign of terror*, was carried out by the new state in an attempt to overturn the workings and systems of the old order. Interestingly, this terrorism was seen as a virtuous endeavour, aimed at protecting liberty and democracy. This is how modern terrorism has some bearing to its historical origins – that is, it is systematic, organized and involves preparation for a purpose – and that this aim or objective is political. However, in today's world of terrorism, the reality is often a lot more haphazard. Ultimately, the French model of state terrorism consumed itself – including Robespierre. More recent examples illustrate the question of message and intent. The Italian Carlo Pisacane, a former duke of San Giovanni, died in 1857 in his efforts to alter Bourbon rule that he had found so morally in decline, naming the idea as *the propaganda of the deed*. It later enhanced the revolutionaries of the late nineteenth century, for example, the Russian Narodnaya Volya, who carried out acts of symbolic terrorism.[6] This included targeting members of the royal family or other noble figures. Irish revolutionaries did much the same until the tail end of the twentieth century. The 'dynamite campaign' was in full swing in London in the late nineteenth century. The intelligence, policing and information-driven campaign to counter this VE led to the first dedicated unit focused on CT known as the Special Branch of Scotland Yard.

Aspects of the model used by Irish 'terrorists' to effect political change still operates today. First, the importance of establishing foreign bases to help prepare, train and develop the instruments of terror away from the prying gazes of the ever-watchful became the norm. This also includes being able to prepare and spread propaganda from these sites. Second, the targeting of mass transport systems, especially the underground, can also be seen in modern terrorism. These actions have no regard for the loss of innocent human life.[7] As anarchism flourished elsewhere in the late nineteenth century, it also came to be known by the use of handbooks or playbooks that informed readers on how to carry out acts of violence. However, as 'much as many contemporary observers similarly denigrate modern-day terrorists as mindless, obsessive, and maladjusted – it was a member of Young Bosnia, Gavrilo Princip, who is widely credited with having set in motion the chain of events that began on 28 June, 1914, when he assassinated the Hapsburg archduke Franz Ferdinand in Sarajevo and culminated in the First World War'.[8]

By the 1930s, the understanding of terrorism changed again. It was less about revolutionary movements and more about returning to the idea of state-orchestrated terrorism, leading to authoritarian regimes in fascist Italy, Nazi Germany and Stalinist Russia. Mussolini regarded terrorism as a form of 'street hygiene', but it became part of Nazi and fascist governance – an arm of the state, extending to a state-sponsored elimination of Jews, communists and other 'undesirables'. After the Second World War, state-sponsored terrorism emerged in South America, in particular in Argentina and Chile during the 1970s and later in Salvador and Guatemala during the 1980s – a rule of terror, with terrorism assigned to non-state actors. A further change occurred in how terrorism evolved – largely encompassing the revolutionary movements of societies throwing away the yoke of colonialism – namely Israel, Kenya, Cyprus and Algeria – and during this time, the notion of 'freedom fighters' became accepted parlance. As Yasser Arafat addressed the UN General Assembly in 1974, he mapped out what he regarded as the essential differences between freedom fighters and terrorists, placing himself and the Palestinian Liberation Organization (PLO) squarely in the first category. The PLO was active during the 1970s, carrying out major aeroplane hijackings and creating a movement around their cause that attracted left-leaning ideologues, activists and scholars. 'The difference between the revolutionary and the terrorist', Arafat stated, 'lies in the reason for which each fights. For whoever stands by a just cause and fights for the freedom and liberation of his land from the invaders, the settlers and the colonialists, cannot possibly be called terrorist.'[9] Throughout the 1960s, 1970s and 1980s, these 'terrorist' groups were viewed through this revolutionary lens. They shared their perspectives with their anticolonial precedents, which also included left-wing Marxist, radical intellectuals and revolutionaries joining forces with the struggle against American global economic hegemony, increasingly seen as an imperial superpower. American interests in Vietnam also gave rise to a much wider anti-American and anti-capitalist perspective.

Also important during the late 1970s and early 1980s was the idea of a global terror network, where individual incidents were seen to be part of a shadowy global conspiracy. It reflected a broader attempt made by an omnipotent aggressor, for example, Russia and, more recently, with the idea of Islamist terrorism. It is important to note that until 1989, the Cold War loomed. The difference between East and West was based on capitalism and communism, whereas today it is perceived in terms of Islam and the West, where Islamist extremism has replaced communism. During the 1980s, several attacks by organizations such as Hezbollah, which was formed out of the Lebanese conflict with Israel in 1983, began to target the American military. It is also during this period that Iraq, Syria, Iran and Libya were involved in external revolutionary projects, including the Caribbean Revolutionary Organization and the Secret Army for the Liberation of Armenia. New terrorism evolved in the early 1990s when classic paramilitary revolutionary tactics combined with the interests of illegal drug cartels in South America. This led to change in the meaning of terrorism to a cluster of non-state actors involved in an all-out conflict with the state, whether in the context of criminality or politico-ideological motivations. But the events of 9/11 reshaped how terrorism was conceived of again and it very much still applies in thinking about terrorism to this day.

On this fateful day in 2001, a series of aeroplanes were hijacked, with high-profile American institutions targeted for greatest impact, causing approximately 3,000 deaths. The emotional response to the tragedy of 9/11 was to introduce the 'war on terror'. 'These enemies hate our freedom' was the line persistently repeated by President George W. Bush. It also led to problematic connections made between Al Qaeda and Saddam Hussein, two very separate and unrelated entities. But after 9/11, Washington was keen to make an association between the two. The attack legitimized attempts to not just seek out the 'evildoers' in Afghanistan but to also focus on Saddam Hussein and the 'weapons of mass destruction' that he was alleged to be piecing together in Iraq. President Bush using ill-advised words such as a *crusade* did not help the matter. Not to be meant to be taken literally, the reality is that in the present climate, the 'war on terror' continues to include not just the radical Islamist world, but also North Korea for its state sponsoring of terrorist attacks and the pursuit of nuclear weapons. The legacy of the 'war on terror' continues to this day, with ongoing conflicts throughout the Middle East that have become inward looking after a series of external interventions. It has also created implications for neighbouring countries such as Pakistan. With all of these concerns in mind, it is clear that there are many issues to deal with when thinking about what is meant by terrorism in the context of a post-9/11 'war on terror' world.

Who defines the terrorist?

Whilst it is important to observe the evolution of terrorism in a historical and contemporary context, the changing nature of these definitions reflects on how terrorism evolves, how it works and what effect it has on society. For example, a Jewish terrorist organization known as the Stern Gang carried out a series of bombings on British targets in Jerusalem in the 1940s. It led to an independence struggle bearing fruit in what is the state of Israel today. However, organizations routinely abandon the notion of terrorism in naming themselves. They are evoking terms such as freedom struggle, or self-defence movements, or indeed righteous vengeance, or that they are deliberately avoiding any notional conflict and focusing on concepts such as Al Qaeda – which means 'the base' – or Aum Shinrikyo (the 'Shining Path'), which carried out sarin gas bombings of the Tokyo subway in the mid-1990s. In all these instances, terrorists see themselves as completely incapable of making any political change to the causes that motivate them except through violence. This course may be against an oppressive state or a majority group who acts violently against a minority group or some international order. Terrorists, however, would argue that the problem is not them but rather the workings of society that cause them to seek some form of retribution. What we call terrorism is entirely a function of those who define it or are defined by those who seek to define themselves in accordance with it or against it for various reasons to do with its acceptance or otherwise.

Having stated this, it does not change the nature of the act itself, which is an attempt to disrupt, dislodge and eventually discredit the institutions or systems that the terrorists or freedom fighters are challenging through their actions. If someone is a victim of an attack, they are more likely to see the perpetrators as terrorists. However, if someone has a degree of sympathy with these very same violent extremists, then they may not regard the act as terrorism at all. The UN struggled to define terrorism in 1972, when some nations rejected the proposal to condemn the violence in Munich against the Israeli Olympic team as a terrorist attack on the basis that the perpetrators were carrying out a struggle for freedom and independence. NATO, however, has taken a much more expansive approach to define terrorism as acts of violence that lead to destruction, damage to property and loss of innocent life in any context in which the public at large is at risk. This distinction remains important to tease out because it affects a subtle question concerning who does the defining and how non-state actors instrumentalize the label of terrorism. It also makes clear that there is a fine line between the notions that one side is a liberator while the other is a violent menace to the existing order. But while there are rules of war that ensure that certain state actors do not transgress basic human issues, for example, in the use of sarin gas, however, both terrorists and state actors have used kidnapping, torturing, extraordinary rendition, dehumanization of the enemy, and deliberately or unwittingly targeting civilian populations.

This is where tricky waters enter the picture. A terrorist act defined by the deed could have at its core an individual with no political or ideological objectives. Is that person a terrorist or not? Certainly, the event has created terror and this was the objective, in part, of the perpetrators. This is where it is possible to see the greatest clarity when attempting to define the act and its impact as one where terrorism has been created or the aims were to create terrorism in its? enactment. Alex Schmid regards terrorism as the following five phenomena: crime, politics, warfare, communication and religious fundamentalism.[10] The issue that remains is the question of research and why is it that there are still huge disagreements as to what terrorism is despite its changing meaning over time, how it is caused, what can be done about it and how is it possible to determine a systematic perspective on this particular phenomenon. Part of the issue is that project funding often dictates what is produced in terms of new ideas and new knowledge, whether it is from one side or the other. This would matter less in independent university or certain think tank settings; however, there is also the risk of ideology and bias creeping in under the radar. Much of the research is also determined by the needs of particular policy directives. In the current domain of the CVE paradigm, particular forces dictate what is to be done and who it speaks to. This also affects the issue of data collection because there are only two primary social science data collection techniques available, although the use of data science in recent years is adding a new dimension to the range of possibilities. Nevertheless, much remains historical, including the use of documentary evidence, for example, case files. Observations are also vehicles for recording the moment. The availability of secondary data through large surveys allows researchers to generalize across population samples at a country level and make statements of significance concerning certain attitudes and values held by this population. Using media sources could lead to the accusation of bias or partisanship. Interviewing, however, is a powerful tool and, if done well, it can lead to significant insights on how certain behaviours and attitudes are developed in context.

There is also the question of intersectionality, as terrorism studies encourage researchers with backgrounds in psychology, international relations, politics, criminology, sociology, anthropology and perhaps even the cybersecurity to consider their perspectives in the light of new research questions. However, scholars such as Richard Jackson take much more of a deliberate focus to research.[11] They argue that there is an element of dictating to the dominant hegemonic discourse about both the causes and solutions to terrorism that prevents scholars from fully engaging with the debates or producing purposive research with long-term impact. Social research into terrorism is not without its problems of bias, prejudice and issues of speaking to the customer funding it rather than to the groups affected by it, which can serve to reproduce the status quo, and as a consequence, legitimize existing modes of domination and subordination. In particular, much of research on terrorism focuses on non-state actors, whereas state actors are usually disregarded, rendering the study of state violence entirely removed from the field of terrorism studies and its related disciplines. This is associated with the fact that so much investment is going into CT, and so the view must be that non-state actor terrorism is the most threatening and one that yields the most in terms of social, political and economic damage to nations put at risk by it. The idea that non-state terrorists have purely psychological problems is also a distraction away from focusing on the probability that most of the young men involved in acts of terrorism are not too dissimilar from most other young men in reality. By focusing on the radicalized mentally unstable jihadi suicide bomber who dreams of seventy-two virgins, a degree of dissonance enters into the picture. So much so that it suggests these people are beyond the pale of humanity. But such is the threat posed by this new form of terrorism, it is given priority focus. As a result, a new set of CT measures are provided legitimacy, including, for example, extraordinary rendition or waterboarding, which have their own major consequences down the line.

With considerable interest in terrorism from many different groups, one would expect a certain element of objectivity that would challenge the dominant hegemon concerning terrorism studies; however, this remains lacking. The reason is that state institutions that have a particular role in questions of national security, foreign policy and in international crime have authority over existing ideas generated on terrorism. In pursuit of the objectives of these governmental organizations concerning CT or CVE policy thinking, an element of critical thinking is lost under the banner of consensus building. The realm of CVE research and policy is in part an attempt to this at a global level. Noted by the UN, and supported by President Obama during its incarnation, the idea of CVE has become an international project with nations committed to delivering national action plans. Connected to these instruments of states are intellectuals and researchers who maintain close links to the security service, policing, crime reduction, and related foreign and domestic policy apparatus of various government departments of nations across the world.

Challenging the dominant hegemon

An important element of this book is in trying to ensure a more open-ended understanding of extremism, radicalization and terrorism underpinned by a process of independent critical thinking but also challenges the assumptions held about these topics. This necessarily means that it is important to reflect deeply on the subject matter but also cast a critical eye over much of what is commonly understood and accepted, in the process introducing new ways of thinking through them. The importance of observing real-world issues by looking beyond the emotional surface-level responses that often monopolize the debate, leading to polarization and ultimately further distancing between different actors, is vital. The need to reconceptualize perspectives on society and issues of terrorism within it, understanding how matters have evolved over various historical and conceptual development phases, but also having enough insight to be able to evaluate and critically assess new issues as they emerge, remains paramount. Many who are interested in terrorism also work in the field, namely in government departments, policing, security or intelligence institutions, public or private. Students of terrorism often aspire to do the same. Although there are numerous books on terrorism, and all go through the question of definition or subject matter discussions related to specific events and outcomes, this book necessarily asks the reader to think about the social realm and in particular the structural factors that shape the nature of complex social relations between human beings. This book also provides the reader with an up-to-date critique of the state of terrorism studies, with examples from across the globe. It provides direction for research and policy thinkers to help learn from the past and not to make same the mistakes of misrecognition and misdirection that can sully any attempt to improve understanding and the practice of eliminating VE. The following chapter looks more closely at the efficacy of state terrorism.

2

State terrorism

The previous chapter addressed the question of defining terrorism. It is clear to see that there is no single accepted definition of an oft-complex and polarizing topic that routinely generates so much emotion and disquiet. This was the case especially during the latter stages of the twentieth century when the issue of jihadi extremism became synonymous with the idea of Muslims and Islam per se. It had the effect of hugely distorting perceptions of a global faith tradition while ignoring the many differences that make up a global Muslim population with local area nuances reflecting questions of migration, ethnicity and citizenship – in majority societies or minority. This chapter continues to centre on the definitions, in particular concerning state actors. The Kashmir question and concerns affecting the Palestinian cause are specific case studies in this chapter.

Terrorism without history

An important aspect to begin with is the question of how the historical dynamics of state terrorism still have a bearing on how we think about non-state actors in the current period. The most important factor to consider is the extent to which state terrorism is eliminated from the discourse on terrorism. Its absence has a distorting effect on non-state actor terrorism, which is largely concentrated on jihadi extremism. This disproportionality affects policymaking in starkly negative directions, especially with the question of how non-state actor terrorism is dealt with. With the exponential growth of academic and policymaker output on the topic of terrorism, very little, if at all, converge on state terrorism. This is especially peculiar given the 'genealogy of the term "terrorism"'.[1] It has been used far more frequently than non-state terrorism – and the number of casualties tends to be greater and often more grievous. The central concerns here are the realm of power, knowledge and politics.[2] That is, the question of who decides what the problem is, what are its main constituents, what can be done about it and who has the authority to introduce interventionist measures are of primary interest. Even the term 'terrorism' 'contains within itself the discursive echoes of state violence, despite its more recently constructed meaning as a descriptor for non-state actions and behaviour'.[3] The omission of state terrorism leads to confusion over the idea of terrorism – and it absolves certain states from being taken to task for their actions. Moreover, '[s]tate terrorism most often employs exactly the same methods – bombings, assassinations, kidnap, torture, and the like – as non-state terrorist groups, even if they can be used more widely and frequently by state actors'.[4] There are numerous examples in this regard, all of which permit the status quo to go about unchecked.

There are several instances of state terrorism and state-sponsored terrorism, including where non-state terrorism flourishes within weakened social and political structures. Kashmir and Palestine are just some of the most prominent. Both bear a direct relationship to the end of the colonial period in what were once British colonies, but now permanently facing various internal conflicts due, arguably, in part to the rapid departure of the British at the end of the Second World War. Arguably, one of the reasons why there is such ambiguity over what terrorism means, in theory, or practice, is that it avoids considering the issue of state terrorism. It masks the possibility that CT measures carried out by states can merge into state terrorism. This amnesia permits the focus on terrorism to remain fixated on present conflicts and disremember the long and complex history of state terrorism, especially since the French Revolution onwards, in the process 'maintaining the dangerous myth of Western exceptionalism'.[5] The greatest concern is that the lack of discussion on state terrorism helps to delegitimize revolutionary movements as justifiable political resistance against oppressive structures. This obfuscation can obscure such issues, 'as regime change, economic sanctions, military base expansion, military occupation, military assistance for strategic partners, and the isolation of disapproved political movements such as Hamas or Hezbollah'.[6]

These perspectives help to isolate how terrorism research can serve to legitimize state terrorism, not merely because the latter is invisible in the discourse of terrorism. It leads to certain limitations to questions that can be asked of independent, objective research, which, in the end, is unable to hold states to account. It naturally lends itself to research that does not necessarily challenge the status quo, which invariably misses out the voices and actions of those who participate in terrorism due to genuine grievances that signal a need for politico-ideological change. The implications are weighty. For example, few scholars dare openly criticize Israeli war crimes against the Palestinians in case it impacts their careers, which is a real possibility, especially in the United States. Some of these concerns are genuinely related to the problem of doing rigorous, independent research into terrorism given how difficult it is to identify 'terrorists' to research on – or it is next to impossible to get hold of official documentation on terrorist cases, some of which may well be ongoing. The disproportionality of what is seen as terrorism or not affects a whole host of social and political relations in society. However, with the current and enduring issues of a lack of consensus on state terrorism, arguably a greater killer that can lead to untold death among societies and nations, the bias will continue to have severe consequences for the academy, research and ordinary people affected by these social fissures everywhere in the world.

While there is a sense that state terrorism does not feature in research to the degree perhaps necessary, there is a discourse that suggests that 'new terrorism', namely violent Islamism, is somehow more lethal than its predecessors. Indeed, the internet has changed the nature of how political violence and terrorism are carried out, moving away from formal networks based on real-world associations towards a virtual web of individual and groups linked by interest or motivation. However, it remains unclear as to whether the current period is more destructive. What remains interesting is that there is a space in which non-state actors operate within states that are either weak or strong; however, such settings can allow only those who adapt to the circumstances to survive or prosper, suggesting strong states have an active role in delegitimizing and countering this new terrorism.[7] An important case in point is terrorism research in the Middle East. Much of the general discourse sees Arabs and Israelis pitted against each other in an endless war. However, its asymmetric origins are rarely addressed, for there are decades of grievances, a sense of injustice, and the denial and dehumanization of 'the other' in pursuit of various nationalist political projects. As one group continues to form an intimidating position relative to a subjugated other, matters will only escalate in these settings. Attempt to centre on the idea of the 'Arab terrorism problem' as central to issues across the Middle East as a whole is a long-running narrative that has been built by various political and institutional designs. The historical origins fixate on land, territory and, therefore, history and identity.

The state of Palestine

Out of Palestine, a former territory of the Ottoman Empire and a British Mandate, the state of Israel formed, leaving a bitter sense of injustice on the part of the Palestinians who have suffered immeasurably but without the wider world able to make a difference to the situation. While one might think that this has biblical origins, its history is rooted in recent periods, namely in the nineteenth century when the Zionist movement began to voice its ambitions concerning the formation of the state of Israel.[8] At the end of that century, Theodor Herzl (a Hungarian activist) promoted a policy to encourage Jewish immigration into the territory while attempting to push Arabs into neighbouring countries. The increasing number of Jews entering

Palestine meant that by 1948, Jews made up one-third of the two million population. While the initial view was that Arabs and Jews could coexist in a plentiful land, later leaders began to support the idea that two sides can never live in one place. With a growing Jewish population, the belief was that Palestine would be insufficient to accommodate fully both Jews and Arabs. As a result, Zionism became extreme. It eventually extended to forcibly removing Arabs from their homes and their lands, using violence and intimidation to subvert the population. In this sense, this form of terrorism is strategic, not reactive.[9] Harm was inflicted through direct violence and structural terrorism. Israel is one of those states where any discussion on terrorism naturally focuses on the Palestinians and rarely ever on the nature of the state itself. However, both sides took to violence as a means to respond to direct conflict, with Jewish casualties higher relative to the Arabs in the early twentieth century, but by its tail end, this relationship had been completely inverted. Throughout this time, Britain continued to support the immigration of Jews and confiscation of land. As the Arabs were forced into the cities, Palestine became fertile ground for rising dissent and anger at the hands of the oppressive other. This fighting grew to the extent that over '5,000 Palestinians and at least 463 Jews were killed in the fighting before British forces crushed the Arab revolt in 1939'.[10] However, Britain's policy concerning the immigration of Jews became restrictive after 1939. In doing so, it was in direct conflict with the Jewish community globally after the end of the Second World War. In July 1946, the Irgun gang (whose commander at the time was Menachem Begum, becoming later the sixth prime minister of Israel from 1977 to 1983) bombed the King David Hotel, killing ninety people.

In 1947, the UN recommended partition; however, the Irgun gang and Lehi militias killed 120 villagers in attacks in April 1948. A retaliation by the Arabs saw the deaths of seventy Jewish medical personnel. Subsequent attacks by Israeli forces led to the flight of 300,000 Arab villagers – but by 1949, a year after the declaration of the state of Israel, around three-quarters of a million Arabs had fled their villages. This was an example of *strategic terrorism*. Over 80 per cent of the Arabs had fled – ensuring that there would no population problem for the new state for years to come. Palestinians were placed in refugee camps in neighbouring countries or continued to exist in reduced number inside Israel. In response, an organized Palestinian resistance only emerged in the 1960s, but the PLO (Palestinian Liberation Organization) was expelled from the West Bank in 1968. The Munich attack in 1972 killed nine Israelis and resulted in the deaths of five *Fedayeen* and after two years, in 1974, a prison exchange led to numerous deaths on both sides. However, Palestinians 'retain rights of self-defense and self-determination in their traditional homeland'.[11] 'Palestinian terrorism', therefore, purportedly serves three purposes. First, it demonstrated a strength of force in being able to strike at the enemy, which helped to galvanize broader Palestinian support. Second, Israeli security was threatened by the actions of weaker opposed groups. Third, the Munich attacks were important in bringing to bear a live, global audience, enabling Palestinians to raise their issues on an international scale and encourage others to rally behind their cause. Over the years, the conflict has raged on – including a war of words. The first *intifada* (uprising) started in 1989 – but by 1994 Yasser Arafat went from 'terrorist' to Nobel peace prize-winner (jointly received with Yitzhak Rabin and Shimon Peres).

Since 1967, Israel has engaged in *structural terrorism* through its settlement project, evoking security concerns as a justification – a ruse to confiscate both private and public land. These settlements rage on and on – and are strategically placed, wilfully separating existing Arab villages. Many settlers are armed zealots who are allocated their housing based on their religious convictions associated with their particular denomination. Over time, Israel's consistent claims that the Palestinians are terrorists have encouraged some who might be sympathetic to the Palestinian cause to turn away because of the negative connotations associated with the term. By extending the idea that these 'Palestinian terrorists' share an ideological conviction based on readings of scripture, the rhetoric can be extended to the greater Middle East, irrespective of the complex social realities facing groups there – and this encourages a neo-conservative alignment. The 1982 invasion of Lebanon by Syria in an attempt to weed out the PLO led to thousands of Arabs killed. It preceded the formation of Hezbollah with the backing of Iran and the Revolutionary Guard. After 9/11, the 'war on terror' has made it easier for Israel to maintain the rhetoric of Palestinians as terrorists – 'the rhetoric of "terror" is itself a mechanism of state terrorism, enabling Israel to consolidate its hold on the territories by emphasizing the need for Israel's "security" in the face of Arab terrorism, while submerging any consideration of the Palestinians' own security concerns'.[12]

Hamas organized a campaign of suicide bombings in 1993 when Israel failed to respond to the threats of violence from extremist Jews who did not want the Oslo peace process to go ahead as it would lead to loss of territory. Hamas considered that they had no other option left but to target civilian populations, however ineffective in reality. They felt that no one in the world was listening to their plight – but by taking measures into their hands, the response is often a greater sense of anger and entitlement on the part of the aggressors. But there was also an element of strategic terrorism in acts of violence carried out by Hamas, namely to dampen tourism to Israel, which hurts the economy, especially in the short run. To solve these seemingly intractable issues, there are important questions to answer. Evoking the term 'terrorism' prevents others everywhere from appreciating the human cost of this conflict. Meanwhile, Palestinians are continuously facing persecution, particularly the 2 million or so imprisoned in Gaza. In attempting to define the difference between state terrorism and non-state terrorism, the dividing line seems to appear to be a question of actor-based (determined by individuals or states) and action-based outcomes (determined by consequences).[13] What separates the two is that state actors are not always prepared to use weapons of mass destruction or to weaponize an ideology, although, in the case of Hitler's Germany and Stalin's Russia, these rules were completely thrown out.

The forgotten struggle of Kashmir

In the shadows of the Himalayas stands the forgotten struggle of the Kashmiris, whose plight remains precarious as India tightens its grip, placing the future of the territory in even more uncertainty and insecurity. When Islam came to the region of Kashmir in the thirteenth century, there was no India or Pakistan. A centre of Buddhist and Hindu religion, art, culture and knowledge, when Islam arrived in Kashmir, so did greater syncretism. However, there was also conflict. The Muslims, the Sikhs and the British battled over the province from the seventeenth to the nineteenth centuries. Hindu rule from the mid-1800s until partition in 1947 led to prevarication on the part of the ruler Hari Singh over the question of whether Kashmir was to succeed to either India or Pakistan. He sided with the former. Since then, Jammu and Kashmir (union territory administered by India) became semi-autonomous until 2019, although both India and Pakistan continued to stake a claim to the territory as a whole. Because of these disputes, both countries went to war in 1947 and 1965 and nearly again in 1999, when an incident in Kargil was ready to explode into nuclear war. While the UN granted a plebiscite to the Kashmiris in 1948, that opportunity has yet to be realized. It leaves the Kashmiris caught between two bitterly opposed neighbours. When tensions mount in the territory, India and Pakistan argue that it is a bilateral matter and the world switches off, leaving the Kashmiris with no voice.

The violent struggles in Kashmir have drawn attention to a rift between two neighbouring countries that has its genesis in the partition of India in 1947. In dividing India, two countries were established not as friendly neighbours but as two competitive nations separated by religion and national political identity. Pakistan faced the unfortunate reality of having to start from scratch, whereas India largely inherited the legal, social and democratic structures the British had left behind. These issues aside, while Kashmir was granted a UN plebiscite to determine its future, neither Pakistan nor India was prepared to let go of a territory deemed an important part of the psyche and memory of each nation. The events in Kashmir since July 2016 have witnessed some of the most heated exchanges between the two political entities, but more importantly, significant civilian casualties in the Kashmir valley. The 2016 curfew lasted for nearly two months, and the extensive use of pellets as well as bullets by the Indian army, combined with operations by India and Pakistan, led to over 70 deaths and over 7,000 injuries. One issue that Kashmiris are opposing is the Israeli-like settlement programmes, which have severely dislodged the Kashmiris from their homes and their lands. Kashmiris face the brunt of a mighty occupying force, which displays all of the characteristics of oppressive regimes, driven by ideology, religion and egoism. External powers disempower groups and then physically remove populations from their historical origins, replacing their memories with new histories in the image of the oppressor. These recent Kashmir clashes have raised to the surface tensions that have been simmering for decades but catalysed by assassinations, reprisals, curfews and various human rights abuses that have resulted in a ban on media and the internet, the shutting down of mosques and vigorously enforcing a closedown of the region in all but name. While Pakistan and India blame each other, it is a largely Muslim majority population of Kashmir that face the brunt of the conflict and the tragedies that unfold daily.

At the end of the Second World War, Britain was unable to hold on to its existing territories and quickly withdrew from various parts of the world. The conflicts in Palestine and Kashmir are the legacy of the hasty departure of the British from once-colonized areas. While there is some peace in Northern Ireland, hard-fought after many years of struggle and strife on all sides, the situations in Palestine and Kashmir remain of concern. One can no longer point the finger to the failed British policies of years gone by, but the lack of international support concerning these fragile hotspots. With a great deal of bias in media and among geopolitical actors and states concerning these sites, the future of these territories is uncertain. Today, a wave of authoritarian populist religious nationalism is sweeping India. The 2019 election placed these paradigms at the heart of the campaign. Now Narendra Modi, a youth member of the Hindu nationalist Rashtriya Swayamsevak Sangh (RSS), which was implicated in the assassination of Mahatma Gandhi in 1948, is compelled to sustain a particular worldview that calls into play the status of Hindu India on a global stage. Over recent years, various institutions of India have been carefully and systematically marginalizing Indian Muslims, some of whom face random mob attacks based on spurious claims of smuggling beef or forcibly converting Hindu women, all of which appeal to the idea of Islam as an invasive and uninvited force. At the same time, Pakistan, now under the leadership of Imran Khan, is still getting to grips with issues of development, cronyism and corruption that have plagued the country for generations. With a population likely to double to 350 million within thirty years, Pakistan faces numerous challenges relating to education, land and property rights, and representation.

While Pakistan provides regional autonomy to Azad Kashmiris, on 5 August 2019 India revoked article 370 of its constitution, which eliminated a range of rights once held as sacrosanct. It is now possible for people from outside of India-occupied Kashmir to purchase property within it, permitting the accumulation of capital by external interests, which is likely to undermine an existing delicate balance in Jammu and Kashmir. While many of the Hindu pundits fled the region in the 1990s due to rising Kashmiri insurgency supported by Pakistan in instances, authority and control persist in the hands of the Hindu minorities. At the time of writing, there are 8 million Muslims surrounded by over 900,000 Indian troops who have faced lockdown since 5 August 2019. All forms of communication, travel, transport and trade are halted. Telephone lines were temporarily opened, allowing Kashmiris to talk to their loved ones inside and outside of the territory for the first time in many months. There are talks of as many as 13,000 young men 'lifted' in the middle of the night and taken to jails, often hundreds of miles away, without the knowledge of their families. Young men who resist on the streets face being pelleted. Those searched and then subsequently found with marks on them are not treated but whisked away to faraway jails. Medical supplies have been dramatically reduced, and the economy has suffered drastically as the main markets remain shut and transport remains limited. Traders, workers and travellers have all lost opportunities. There seems to be a concerted effort to break the will of the Kashmiris who have continued to face the tragedies of occupation for over seventy years.

The tensions in the region are affecting Kashmiris in the diaspora. Nearer home, the UK has the largest diaspora of Kashmiris in the world. There are approximately three-quarters of a million Azad Kashmiris across the country, with concentrations in the Midlands and the south. But there are only approximately 500 Kashmiri families in the UK. The vast majority of the British Azad Kashmiris herald from Mirpur. They were originally displaced in the 1960s due to the building of Mangla Dam, which submerged over 200 villages and hence moved many, with a significant number moving to the UK. However, many of these Mirpuris are not recognized as Kashmiris, being reminded that they are Pakistani. But many Azad Kashmiris reject the title of Pakistani. They argue that Pakistan has done little or nothing for the Azad Kashmiris in reality. They are therefore many Kashmiris caught between different identities. Political demonstrations over the recent events in Kashmir in the major cities of the UK often become a stage for some to concentrate on the idea that it is a conflict between India and Pakistan, further silencing the voice of the Kashmiris.

There is a powerful argument put forward by some that the idea of new terrorism is somehow different from old terrorism, and more brutal than the old. In effect, while the brutality associated with suicide bombings and beheadings creates a great deal of emotion, it tends to be highly localized. However, this emphasis on the brutalization of terror takes attention away from the fact that in the 1970s and 1980s, a great deal of state and non-state terrorism inflicted more harm, more deaths and greater instability in societies.[14] Many sources suggest that matters became worse after 9/11, which was a particular turning point in the brutalization of terrorism. However, this is somewhat of an overstatement and evidence suggests that it is far from the case. Moreover, it gives succour to groups who would rather suggest that this new terrorism is religious, or certainly inspired by religious convictions. There is a view which sustains that new terrorism is horizontally structured, while old terrorism was hierarchical – again, this is more conceptual rather than borne out by the evidence. The Global Terrorism Database is a useful tool that enables this question to be investigated empirically. While there has been an increase in beheadings and suicide bombings, the relative proportion of these acts of terrorism is small. There a fixation on the idea that religious perspectives define this new terrorism. However, much of what happens in this arena is determined by superficial understandings, often with deep political underpinnings, arguably to take attention away from genuine failings over what might be driving terrorism in reality. Having introduced the debates on defining terrorism and in why state terrorism is persistently off the radar of scholars and analysts, the following chapter explores ideas relating to the counter-terror state and its practices.

3

The counter-terror state

The cases of Kashmir and Palestine as issues of state terrorism and political violence were discussed in the previous chapter. This chapter extends the broader conceptual framework concerning the question of the role of the state in political violence. The present uneasiness over the nature of CT carried out by nations in the global north has emerged in the context of the 'war on terror' that began after the events of 9/11. The prevailing paradigm has been for numerous states to securitize their societies by promoting military and security discourses. Aspects of social policy, for example in education, border and immigration controls and health, are increasingly being seen within the realm of security.[1] This securitization ensures that the predominant themes of such counter-terror state approaches are to challenge an enduring threat that is seen as merciless in its purpose.[2] The state, rather than individuals, is seen as the primary victim of terrorism, with counter-terror states framing terrorism as a threat to freedoms, values and democracy.[3] This framework exists as rationalization for the implementation of counter-terror measures. The introduction of legislation to exert state power normalizes and legitimizes state attempts to limit the dangers of terrorism from non-state actors.[4] Governments, media, financial institutions and academia reproduce the framing of the threat in such states.[5] The counter-terror state, through the process of securitization, produces repression in society. In the global north, in particular, much of these issues affect Muslim minority groups dealing with the structural asymmetry that counter-terror state creates.[6]

Radicalization and (in)security

'Radicalization' is a complex and multi-layered term. It is both a *process* and an *outcome*. The term helps to capture the processes through which individuals move from an initial stage of becoming an extremist to eventually engaging in terrorism and political violence. But it operates in multiple directions, such that a radicalized individual may choose not to advance their convictions to the point they turn violent. At some level, their desire not to engage in VE is a form of redirected radicalization or de-radicalization through self-awareness. The universality of the concept of radicalization suggests a consensus regarding what is meant by the term and its usage; however, the modern application of the concept has only been established in recent periods. It has resulted in different approaches on what it means and how it is used, in the process creating create confusion and misunderstanding. It can be interpreted within a context of security, integration or foreign policy.[7] Since radicalization, seen through the security lens framing, is considered a threat to the security of the state, radicalization is interpreted as characteristically preceding terrorism. In these instances, where terrorism represents a unique and critical threat, the fight against terrorism, CT, can create conditions that suppress essential human and civil rights.[8] The weakening of civil rights is seen as acceptable in the fight against terrorism, where the severity of terrorist attacks serves as the reason for the deterioration of civil liberties. In this regard, first, the establishment of CT is far-reaching and usually endless, where incremental changes to policy are rarely abrogated. Second, CT policies can result in innocent civilians being detained, tortured or killed. In some instances, civilians are considered collateral damage in counter-terror operations.[9] Counter-terrorism agencies concentrate on results rather than actions, with less evidence needed to arrest or detain people than in ordinary circumstances. It increases the likelihood of innocent people being unfairly accused and prosecuted. The emphasis on suspicion provides the counter-terror state more leeway in the implementation of policy. This can be observed in the military dimension of CT, where 'signature strikes' afford drones more freedom to decide when and where to carry out attacks. Targets can be selected based on suspicious behaviour alone, hugely increasing the risk of collateral damage represented in the deaths of innocent civilians.[10] Third, the established CT legislation can place fundamental democratic principles in jeopardy. A right to a fair trial and the right to privacy are examples of basic principles that can be violated. The state, the most crucial provider of security, cannot guarantee these fundamental freedoms in prioritizing CT policy. Thus, states have the legislative capacity and resources to create far more disruption for an entire population than a single terrorist actor could ever realize.

Radicalization is a *process*, as an *outcome* and an *experience*.[11] In parallel to the question of political violence, where political ideology inspires individuals to violence, the idea of radicalization is also being evoked in the context of a 'war on terror culture', including where there is a role to play for the CT, counter-radicalization or even counter-extremism industries. The origin of radicalization is the term 'radical', which, in the political sense, is used to refer to the desire to bring about radical democratic reforms. Today, the concept of radicalization is largely perceived to act as a window into violence and destruction. However, in the CT realm, the dominant view is to argue that it is possible to moderate this radicalization through various interventions – and that these are about shifting people away from religious or political ideologies that might lead individuals to violence. Radicalism, therefore, is an analytical concept, which has application within the social sciences. And herein lies the problem, because neither radicalization nor radicalism always refers to violence. The presence of individuals possessing various political, religious or ideological beliefs does not necessarily suggest that they are on a path towards violence as a means reveal radical political or social outcomes. In the study of radicalization, a focus on contextual matters is essential but the importance of the micro-level, where the individual faces a series of complexities that lead to vulnerabilities, which subsequently generate the susceptibilities that might lead to violence, remain the key point of interest for the research, policy and practice realm.

Warring against terror

The 'war on terror' began after the events of 9/11. At the time, given the horrific nature of the 9/11 attacks, the United States and its allies engaged in a programme of containment, first in Afghanistan and then quickly in Iraq, which was deemed to be part of the 'axis of evil' consisting of Iran, Iraq and North Korea. The idea of the 'war on terror' was to engage rapidly in response to the events in New York and Washington DC on the fateful September day in 2001. By establishing US military bases in Afghanistan and Iraq as well as ensuring that these regimes were pro-United States concerning the democratic systems and economic outlook that would emerge in the aftermath, the United States hoped to achieve a response that led to it being seen as the world's strongest global player. This was the plan. However, it did not bear the intended fruit. The fact that the 'war on terror' rages on in all but name suggests either that the original policy was wrong or that the means have been problematic. The very nature of the response by the United States deepened the conditions that give rise to Islamist radicalization across the world.

In the 1980s, the Soviet invasion of Afghanistan resulted in the emergence of Sunni rebels, who were seen as freedom fighters. They were trained initially by the CIA with the support of the Pakistani ISI (Inter-Service Intelligence). Many from across Central Asia and the Middle East joined what was seen as a legitimate struggle in Islam, weaponizing ideology as an instrument of US foreign policy. Of the many young idealistic men join, one was Osama bin Laden and another Ayman al-Zawahiri. Both were influenced by the writings of Sayid Qutb and the goal of establishing a global Muslim front in resistance to what they saw as the decaying morals of the West and the ever-encroaching attempts made by foreign powers to meddle in the Muslim world. They evoked a vision of a perfect social, economic, legal and political system devoid of any semblance of impurity – a land for Muslims by Muslims inspired by the teaching of a purer Islam, as they saw it. After 1991 when the

Soviet Union collapsed, many fighters returned to their home countries; however, some stayed. Bin Laden was prevented from remaining in Saudi Arabia as he was seen as a security risk. His increasingly hostile views towards the Saudi Arabian state and the ruling elite, the royal House of Saud, made them anxious. Bin Laden subsequently went to Khartoum in Sudan, where he was able to spread his message, now intent on galvanizing Muslim support across the Islamic world to resist occupation by external forces, including in Saudi Arabia, which he had seen to be under the yoke of the United States.[12]

Meanwhile, as Afghanistan descended into civil war in the early 1990s, the Taliban sought to resist infighting, but later the Taliban was radicalized by a much more virulent strain of Islamism. In 1998, US domestic missions were shelled in Nigeria and Kenya. In 2000, the USS Cole was bombed off the coast of Eden. At the end of the 1990s, the Taliban was operating various terrorist training camps throughout the non-governable areas of Afghanistan. From this emerged the idea of Al Qaeda, which in Arabic means 'the base' – a loose affiliation of an international network of like-minded radical Sunni rebels who were prepared to militarize their political ambitions concerning an end of times thesis and the desire to introduce a global sharia system. Its focus was the Middle East and Israel, but there were also extensions into areas such as Chechnya, Thailand as well as Indonesia and increasingly Pakistan, which was beginning to dangle its tentacles into Islamization, especially after General Zia Ul Haq introduced various pro-Islamic reforms during a military dictatorship that spanned the 1980s. Therefore, it is important to see the attacks of 9/11 within this light. They were an attempt by an organization to spread a global message by striking the primary economic, political and military institutions of the United States. Al Qaeda was anticipating that the United States would carry out a sustained response to this event, and so the attack was a calculated event, aimed at ensuring that a global effort in the battle of the end of times would encourage widespread Muslim engagement.

Counter-terrorism backfiring

Meanwhile, back in the United States, a powerful body of neoconservative Republicans organized what became the project known as the New American Century. It argued that the United States has a responsibility to lead the globe, arguably in response to the perceived notion that Bill Clinton's America was unable to take advantage of the fall of the Soviet empire. This body of people included Vice President Dick Cheney, his Chief of Staff Lewis Libby, Defense Secretary Donald Rumsfeld and Deputy Defense Secretary Paul Wolfowitz, as well as John Bolton at the State Department. While Afghanistan capitulated relatively quickly, with the Taliban dispersed, and although Iraq fell early on, it subsequently led to huge disruption across the entire region and beyond. Attacks by Al Qaeda continued around the world, including in Turkey, Indonesia, Saudi Arabia, with consulates and embassies attacked in particular. In 2004, the Madrid train bombings, and in 2005 the events of 77 in London, brought terrorism to the heart of European cities. As this violence peaked in 2007 and then plateaued until 2012, a whole host of instabilities began to be observed across the Middle East. The Arab Spring that began in 2011 emerged within the context of these ongoing conflicts.

Boko Haram emerged in Nigeria in 2002, and it continues to cause havoc in the country, especially as it aligned itself to Islamic State in 2015. Al-Shabab has grown as a threat in Kenya and Tanzania and remains active to this day. All of this local radicalization emerged in the light of the 'war on terror', which was seen as an attempt, at first, to break down a hierarchical, networked organization with a single core leader at the centre. Over time, a range of affiliates emerged, including those who espoused similar aspirations and motivations, as well as the means in terms of their logistics and organizational capacities, to reproduce the rhetoric that originally grew through the formation of Al Qaeda. The US assumption about the 'war on terror' was that by removing, Osama Bin Laden, *the head of the snake*, the entire system would collapse. It presumed a structural organizational capacity to Al Qaeda, which was, in part, overstated quite considerably for effect. As a movement that began in the late 1980s, Al Qaeda had the elements of 'consortium, franchise and network'.[13] Those inspired by the rhetoric of Al Qaeda wished to emulate its ambitions, suggesting a transnational movement. The Arab Spring was an attempt for countries struggling with tribalism, uneven development, cronyism, militarism and deep-seated structural inequalities to engage in various social revolutionary movements that could act as a wedge against the ambitions of organizations such as Al Qaeda. However, the failure of the Arab Spring led to the emergence of newly formed radical militarized Islamist groups, leading to a new wave of violence and destruction; in particular, the rise of the Islamic State in 2013.

The Islamic State is no longer a potent force. However, conflict rages on in parts of Iraq and Syria for a whole host of reasons to do with governance, democracy and political reform. The US 'war on terror' was a direct response to the Al Qaeda attacks, but it was designed by a political project, the aim being to maintain America's position as a global authority, politically, culturally and economically. But this response was disproportionate and politico-ideologically motivated, especially when the introduction of the 'axis of evil' is considered, which can be seen as an attempt to ratchet up the nature of the conflict and its reach much further than the original intentions. As the 'war on terror' moved beyond Afghanistan, with attention shifting to the Middle East, the country remains deeply mired in conflict, with external actors still on the ground intending to restore some notion of governance, including in often-lawless regions of the country. Yet, while direct combat based on traditional models of armed warfare has subsided in recent years, they have been replaced with drones, the use of third-party private contractors and other means of control.

A faceless killing

The question remains whether the current ongoing approach has any real bearing in shifting the nature of the conflict in these parts of the world, or whether in fact, its perpetuation maintains the inequities and injustices that people feel which cause some to be drawn to various violent revolutionary social movements. This is important to consider given the changing nature of warfare. No longer are soldiers required to wage war on the ground. Drones operated out of New Mexico, but attacking targets in such places as Afghanistan, have become a weapon of war. These drone programmes are both biopolitical and necropolitical – where, in this case, an external power, namely US-led forces, determines who among the population deserves to live or die. Research demonstrates that drone programmes radicalize people who are under its surveillance, not prevent its further growth.[14] The language of those who espouse the drone programme reproduces a system of state terrorism that can be read through the ideas of Orientalism. Drones do not have emotions in the way that humans do – which can make them effective killing machines. To promote the idea of these drones, states emphasize the importance of the accuracy of drone targeting, such that killing has become an efficient act of war – an ethical solution to 'collateral damage', no less. It forges a link between surveillance, control and elimination of populations. Those who perpetuate it argue that drone killing is somehow more humane. However, drone programmes are biopolitical. The language is neo-colonial, often filled with racist stereotypes. Moreover, its necropolitical rationality transforms into state terrorism, such that 'the rhetoric that idealises US violence omits how surveillance and drone use is predicated on racism and imperial domination, and how it necessarily brutalises and renders killable those being observed'.[15]

This expansion of the drone programme developed dramatically after the end of President W. George Bush's regime and the emergence of the President Obama era in 2008. It was Obama who relentlessly pursued Osama bin Laden, overseeing the successful assassination of America's number one foe in Pakistan in 2011. Did the Obama regime, therefore, continue the 'war on terror' in all but name? By doing so have both US foreign policy and the effect it has on the Muslim world remained in the same direction? Obama's language was to essentially maintain the 'war on terror' but to take attention away from the negative associations it carried.[16] Under President Trump, the 'war on terror' maintained the direction of the prior hegemonic CT discourse. Both Iran and North Korea remain firmly on the 'axis of evil'.

In the post-9/11 'war on terror' era, to achieve US-led objectives, the landscape of counterinsurgency has expanded with implications, which opens up the discussion on using self-defence as a reason to sidestep human rights. However, despite the lives of non-combatant civilians at stake, drones are still considered a necessary option for their efficiency. With these new tactics and advanced technology at their disposal, drones offer a simple solution. But the Orientalist gaze combined with the legitimization of biopolitics is a product of racism. It creates a hierarchy of human lives. With insensitive statements from US officials and the framing of collateral damage as proportional to the deaths on 9/11, the lives of ordinary citizens who are killed are perceived necessary for preserving US security. Similarly, the use of drones is a license to kill, as people suspected of terrorism are not seen as human beings. Even if using drones for signature strikes were halted, the repressive elements of surveillance do not ease. While drones provide knowledge for intelligence analysts, orientalist attitudes cannot be easily erased since they do not exist in a vacuum. The concept of state terrorism is discussed further when the topic of ethnic cleansing is considered in the following chapter.

4

Genocide and ethnic cleansing

The ideas of necropolitics and biopolitics help can explain aspects of global CT or the role of the counter-terror state globally. Over the years, their changing meaning, in particular, concerns around state violence and experiences of minority groups undergoing processes of radicalization, combined with the ongoing 'war on terror', are indicative of the importance of acknowledging the central roles of states. This chapter explores the question of genocide as another example of state terrorism, and in particular, the significance of ethnic cleansing, with recent examples used to help illuminate discussion on this topic. There are numerous examples that emerge of how various hyper-nationalist programmes have attempted to eliminate a population, particularly by targeting Muslim minority groups. This is not necessarily born out of hatred towards a minority group. Rather, it serves the purposes of ethnic nationalism, which is often interlaced with religion, as in the case of Israel, India, Northern Ireland and Myanmar. In many ways, genocide is state terrorism – of both the strategic *and* structural type.

Genocides continue in different forms despite attempts to better understand and address their causes. But is genocide a particular method of political violence that seeks to annihilate a particular national, ethnic, religious or minority group? What is the nature of the relationship between the political, cultural and ideological in shaping genocides in history? How do recent genocides differ from historical cases? Should the massacre of Rohingyas in Myanmar be classed as genocide? What does the UN Security Council say on genocide? These and other questions are addressed in this chapter.

Genocide as hyper-ethnic nationalism

When more than a million Armenians died during the First World War, the term 'genocide' itself was not yet formulated. With the Holocaust, six million Jews and other minorities were killed, and so in the 1940s Raphael Lemkin, who was a Polish jurist, coined the word 'genocide'. The word is made up of the Greek 'genos', which means people, and the word 'cide', which stands for murder, in short, the 'murder of a people'.[1] In 1948, the United Nations enacted the *Convention on the Prevention and Punishment of the Crime of Genocide*, defining genocide thus:[2]

> Article II
> In the present Convention, genocide means any of the following acts committed with intent to destroy, in whole or in part, a national, ethnical, racial or religious group, as such:
> (a) Killing members of the group;
> (b) Causing serious bodily or mental harm to members of the group;
> (c) Deliberately inflicting on the group conditions of life calculated to bring about its physical destruction in whole or in part;
> (d) Imposing measures intended to prevent births within the group;
> (e) Forcibly transferring children of the group to another group.

If a party acts with the intention to destroy a protected group in whole or in part, they are committing genocide. When a state is committing genocide, one could argue that it is a form of state terrorism. Terrorism is an act of violence towards a target group with the sole purpose to destroy the will of that group. When a state commits an act of genocide against a particular group or another state, it can lose all legitimacy and acceptance.[3] But with the multitude of so many possible crimes in just one word, such a broad term leads to discussions about its application. It is possible, for example, to argue that the intention is to destroy all the people? The primary objective could be something entirely different, and the acts described in Article II might, therefore, be no part of a genocide.[4] However, even if it was not the intention to commit it in the first instance, 'genocidal destruction is the transformation of the victims into "nothing" and the survivors into "nobodies".[5] The targeted group disappears, materially as well as symbolically. Survivors are forced to forget who they were, rendering genocide not simply a reality of killing a body of people, but also referring to erasing them from history.

Nationalism exists in many different forms, but it is essentially a set of ideas, principles or a belief about the history and memory of a nation. This principle can, for instance, combine political objectives with cultural beliefs to justify the protection of a nation's set of rights as an ideal. Generally, nationalism contains two main principles: territorial borders are defined, and can be controlled; and, second, boundaries are defined concerning the membership of the population that contains the nation.[6] Once a movement emphasizes the second element of nationalism, on defining the boundaries of membership by narrowing its definition to a particular ethnicity, one can speak of ethnic nationalism, where political actors justify their policy through 'the interests of the nation defined in ethnic terms'.[7] An ethnic group has a common culture while a racial group lays claim to shared blood, but both groups have a belief in common descent, leading to claims relating to particular territories. In what one sees as culture exists the allusion to a common history, often a shared religion, as well as familiar language and symbols. The group has a 'will' to be a group, and feels threatened by other groups with their own respective 'wills' that regard their group as both unitary and unique.

It is undoubtedly the case that one cannot look at genocide without considering the histories of imperialism, colonialism, slavery and nation-building. One of the most significant recent historical events is the Holocaust, but since then states have committed as many as fifty genocides. However, the Holocaust should not be seen as a singular event in history, but rather a continuation that stretches from the dawn of time. A particular problem of singling out the Holocaust is that it can often act as screening against criticism of contemporary Israeli policies, given historical precedents after the Second World War and the formation of Israel out of existing mixed ethnic and religious populations in 1948. The notion of anti-Semitism also enters into the mix. Thus, it is necessary not to introduce a hierarchy of victimization and this is why the importance of comparative genocide studies comes into play. Verily a particular memory associated with the Holocaust exists, as well as the implications it raised for the Jewish population of the world, but genocide studies allow one to concentrate on a range of related discussions.[8]

The denials of state terror

Too many states are in denial about historical genocides; for example, Turkey concerning the Armenian genocide of the early twentieth century. This topic remains a sore issue for Turkish nationalists, and open criticism can lead to prosecution at the hands of the Turkish state. It reflects disaffirmation where the internet can easily promulgate false information, for example, Holocaust denial or the trivialization of Nazi crimes. Denial thrives in a culture of ignorance, which can become the resignations of an entire society and the knowledge of its past. It prevents victims from obtaining justice. It prevents scholars the ability to document the truth.[9]

Ethnic cleansing, where civilian populations are forcibly transported from an area or killed on ethnic or religious grounds, is in some ways related to genocide as both concern the potential annihilation of populations. In recent periods, the concept is commonly associated with the events in the former Yugoslavia during the mid-1990s. Again, this is not a new phenomenon, as attested by the experience of the Jews, who were banished 'from England (1290), France (1306), Hungary (1349–1360), Provence (1349 and 1490), Austria (1421), Lithuania (1445), Cracow (1494), Portugal (1497), numerous German principalities at various times, and Russia (1724). Spain expelled its Jews in 1492'.[10] European colonizers used ethnic cleansing during the seventeenth and eighteenth centuries, with forced exile as the dominating motif. In 1947, India was partitioned into two, forcing Muslims in one direction and Hindus to the other. Partition occurred in Cyprus in 1974, when both Greece and Turkey invaded, leading to an end of the mixing of existing populations. In the former Yugoslavia, new nation-states have emerged based on specific ethnic and religious categories once under the rubric of 'Yugoslavia', when communities once lived in far more mixed circumstances. What is driving these conflicts? What are the conditions in which these kinds of conflicts emerge readily? Social scientists have been concerned with the connection between economic inequality and civil wars. Societies that exhibit greater ethnic divisions are more likely to demonstrate cleavages that might lead to social conflict. Therefore, '[a]ddressing political inequality and the maintenance of an equitable social contract between the governors and the governed must go hand in hand with rectifying economic grievances'.[11]

The major determinant of ethnic cleansing for political violence towards minority groups is based on the question of nationalism and the idea of an imagined community.[12] While much of the twentieth century contains numerous examples of genocide, the preconditions for ethnic cleansing focus on two types of nationalism. One is the cultural variation and the other is based on the political and social context. This is the difference between civic nationalism and ethnic nationalism; with the latter the main element a driver of ethnic cleansing in recent periods. Pressure by the state to encourage minorities to assimilate can have negative consequences. When such groups do not always meet the requirements of the state, they can be scapegoated by the state, especially when issues of social conflict are indications of ethno-religious conflict.[13]

Given the brutality of genocide and ethnic cleansing, are race and racism at the heart of motivations, ideologies and practices of various states concerning minority groups within existing territories? This does apply in most settings unless it is autogenocide. Alternatively, is the ideological construction of an undesirable minority group painted as a particular problem for and even danger to majorities within these very same territories? This does seem to be borne out in many instances, past and present. Therefore, the logic of genocide and ethnic cleansing could well be explained by simple notions of prejudice, combined with nation-building. In effect, it is racism on an international scale. In all cases, the central importance of intent is clear. The actions are deliberate. The consequences are calculated. Eliminations of certain populations permit the formalization of the binary distinctions that make up the notion of insider and outsider, us and them, citizen or mere temporary denizen. Moreover, '[g]enocide is more likely to occur when it is grounded in an identity construction process in which political elites reconstruct the identities of their victims as a threatening "enemy within".[14] Colonialism, nationalism, scientific racism and globalization have aggrandized issues of ethnic nationalism as they all resist civic nationalism. It results in people looking in narrower terms for whom they can regard as sufficiently part of the 'self' in exclusion of the 'other'.[15]

Killing Muslims

Kashmir

The historical origins of the Kashmiri conflict lie in the formation of both India and Pakistan. Two nations were founded from the partition of India in 1947. Acts carried out in haste by the last Viceroy of India, Lord Louis Mountbatten, in an attempt to quit India quickly after the Second World War when it was no longer a viable entity for the now-faded empire, led to the forced exile of over ten million people but also the ongoing disputes over Kashmir between these two new nations. This territory is fundamental to notions of nationhood for both India and Pakistan – both see it as crucial to the formation of their nations – hence, its absence creates the trauma that produces the basis for VE among some. In many ways, the conflict in Kashmir relates to the idea of the Great Game that engulfed Russia, Iran and Britain and their various attempts to control the routes into and out of the Northwest Frontier. For the British, Kashmir was where numerous empires met – the Persians, Afghans, Chinese and the Russians.

Pakistan and India lay claim to Kashmir for different reasons. 'Early pro-Pakistan accounts presented the Kashmir dispute within the 'two-nation theory'. Religious bonds, geographical position, economic ties, transport and communication links – "all indicated Kashmir's natural integration with Pakistan".[16] However, 'Indian accounts, on the other hand, [have] approached Kashmir from a grand self-perception of a syncretic India and, [while] highlighting Kashmir's legal accession to India, [have] charged Pakistan with aiding and abetting an invasion of Indian territory.'[17] While this game was being played out, with the British in particular wanting to ensure that they had a hand in what came next in that part of the world, Kashmir split between two emerging nations, with both laying claims to claims over its provenance. It has led to, 'one million Kashmiri Muslim refugees [being] uprooted and an estimated 2,500,00–300,000 were massacred in the Jammu region alone in August-October 1947'.[18] These Muslim groups were pushed out under duress – which, could be characterized as ethnic cleansing. Kashmir was divided into two types of Muslims – those in soon to be Azad Kashmir, liberated by Pakistan, and who had Punjabi influences, were in favour of joining Pakistan after partition. In Jammu – the Indian side and with the greater population – the people spoke Kashmiri, but its leader, Hari Singh, favoured alignment with India. The failure to take into account the opinions of Kashmiris during the partition and the following wars between India and Pakistan (1947, 1965, 1998–9) has created lines of division across the landscape of Kashmir which have resulted in the militarization of the valley replete with terror, insecurity and political strife.[19] The latter has reached new heights since the revoking of Article 350 of the Indian constitution in August 2019, rendering obsolete the special status of Jammu and Kashmir.

For the Kashmiri Muslims, who since the late 1980s have lost 70,000 due to the conflict, theirs is a *push* towards violence, which is based on addressing historical grievances, as opposed to the idea that it is a *pull* – one that is necessarily aiming to attain something new or quite different. It is also clear that biases in Indian society prevent its two hundred million Muslims from achieving levels of education and social mobility normally experienced by the majority populations. In recent periods, India has drifted further to the right concerning religious nationalism, which is re-imagining a narrow Hinduistic past for the country today, but it is done so at the expense of demonizing an internal population that has been part of the territory for at least a thousand years. In Indian-held Kashmir, Muslims make up two-thirds of the population, yet their education and labour market outcomes reflect the general positions of Indian Muslims per se.[20] These Muslims are less well qualified than the Kashmiri average and are more likely to be undertaking agricultural or other low-skilled work. Muslims in Kashmir are more likely to be non-workers than non-Muslims.[21]

Former Yugoslavia

In 1948, Josip Broz Tito broke Yugoslavia from Russia, establishing a variation of socialism and an independent communist state. After Tito died in 1980, issues began to emerge in Yugoslavia, including ethnic tensions between groups who felt increasingly unequal to each other. By August 1990, Serbian uprisings in Croatia were being documented. In 1991, Slovenia and Croatia became independent states. The 1991 conflict that engulfed Croatia was entering Bosnia-Herzegovina in 1992. This is when first accounts of 'ethnic cleansing' emerged, placing Europe into a state of shock. While all sides forcibly moved populations, Serbs had the greatest role in displacing Slavic Muslims.[22] In particular, the scenes from Srebrenica are the most telling of all.

Tens of thousands of Bosnian Muslims took refuge in Srebrenica after fleeing from Bosnian Serb attacks in other parts of the country. In

April 1993, the UN Security Council designated Srebrenica a 'safe area' from hostile attack, protected by a lightly armed Dutch peacekeeping battalion. However, for three years, Bosnian Serb troops laid siege to the town, encircling it and subjecting the civilian population to constant military assaults, including shelling, shooting and occasional bombing. In the lead-up to July 1995, even more Bosnian Serb artillery and tanks advanced towards Srebrenica, until around 5,000 troops surrounded the town, with around twenty tanks and other battle vehicles.

On 6 July, Bosnian Serb troops launched a full-scale offensive on Srebrenica, heavily shelling civilian targets over the next few days. On 11 July, Bosnian Serb troops led by Ratko Mladić entered the town, causing UN peacekeepers and several thousand Bosnian Muslims, mostly women and children, to flee to the peacekeeping force's compound on Srebrenica's outskirts. Bosnian Serb troops started forcibly bussing Bosnian Muslims out, as well as separating men and boys from their families. In the following days, approximately 8,000 men and boys were massacred and left in mass graves across Srebrenica.

This targeting emerged from Serbian nationalist ambitions, with the presence of Bosnian Muslims posing an apparent threat to the 'greater Serbian' project. Slobodan Milošević controlled Serb media, which was used to disseminate his nationalist propaganda. Despite Bosnian Muslim groups being largely secular, the Serb media, political and cultural narrative emphasized religiosity. Notably, nationalist ideology defined Serb identity through reference to the 1389 defeat of the Serbs by Turkish Muslims from the invading Ottoman army during the Battle of Kosovo. This provided a basis for the 'othering' of Muslims in Serb society, compounded by the Serbian media's repeated use of pejorative terminology to describe Muslims, including 'Mujahedin fighters', 'balijas' and 'fundamentalist warriors of jihad' and – drawing on the historic Ottoman invasion – 'Turks'.

Rape and sexual violence were key features of the Bosnian conflict, perpetrated by men from all sides. Bosnian Serb forces used rape systematically as part of their ethnic cleansing campaign, with tens of thousands of women estimated to have been raped. They set up so-called rape camps where Bosnian Muslim women and girls were gang-raped, tortured and forcibly impregnated by soldiers and paramilitaries, some daily. The rapists made their anti-Muslim intent clear by cursing the women as 'balija mothers' and 'Turks' as they brutally defiled them. The accounts from abused women are still being documented, with *Surviving the Genocide* (2011), one of many.[23] Within the Serbian project of cultural and biological annihilation, gender informed the goals of genocide in several specific ways. While Bosnian Muslim men were enslaved, tortured, mutilated and killed, women were enslaved, sexually violated tormented mutilated, impregnated and, in some cases, murdered.[24]

Myanmar

A contemporary case studies of genocide and ethnic cleansing refer to the experience of the Rohingya – an issue that rages on to this day. The Rohingya are an ethnic minority group in Myanmar of predominantly Muslim faith. They have suffered decades of discrimination and human rights violations by the Myanmar government, including denial of citizenship.[25] Successive Burmese governments have dismissed the existence of the Rohingya as an ethnic group in Myanmar, instead referring to them as 'illegal immigrants' from Bangladesh or 'Bengalis'.[26]

Anti-Muslim sentiment has risen in Myanmar in recent years. Reuters conducted an investigative report that recorded more than a thousand examples of social media posts, comments, images and videos attacking the Rohingya and other Muslims, almost entirely in the Myanmar language. It appears as though a deliberate anti-Muslim narrative is being constructed to form the nationalist Buddhist perspective, implicating Buddhist monks, the military and ordinary citizens. They have responded to perceived threats to Buddhist culture with increased nationalist and anti-Muslim rhetoric, establishing a narrative in which Muslims seek to 'take over' Myanmar through marriage via the conversion of Muslim women.[27]

In 2017, the Arakan Rohingya Salvation Army (ARSA), a Rohingya insurgency group, launched coordinated attacks on police posts and an army base. ARSA claimed to be taking 'defensive actions' in at least twenty-five locations. Purportedly in response to these attacks, the Burmese Army embarked upon 'clearance operations' against Rohingya villages, which reportedly included the destruction of hundreds of villages, the killing of up to 10,000 Rohingya civilians, mass rapes and the deportation of up to 100,000 Rohingya to Bangladesh. In many villages, the attacks took the following pattern: men were summarily killed while the women were systematically raped.[28] This is another example of ethnic cleansing but is it also genocide? The Gambia considers it is and has filed a complaint of genocide against Myanmar before the UN's International Court of Justice. The Court has granted provisional measures for Myanmar to comply with its obligations under the Genocide Convention. While this is not a final determination of whether genocide has been committed, it is a small symbolic victory for the Rohingya. The systematic elimination of the Rohingya has been centrally planned – in many ways, experiencing similar realities to Kashmiris and Palestinians. This is not a question of Buddhist–Muslim relations, but a question of power, opportunity and nationalism. It has been 'a slow-burning genocide' for thirty-five years.[29]

Having looked at issues of definitions of terrorism, state violence, the counter-terror state and underlying issues relating to ethnic cleansing and genocide to establish the grounds concerning a discussion on political violence, the following part explores the nature of how to deal with the particular issue of radicalization and de-radicalization as a concern for policymaking in particular.

Part Two

Disentangling violent extremism

5

Individual factors in terrorism

Why do people turn to terrorism? Many CVE experts and researchers are preoccupied with identifying the 'drivers' of VE to inform the design and implementation of programmes. However, understanding the factors of VE arguably rework older debates over the 'root causes' of terrorism, which have been controversial in the past because they connoted that terrorism had legitimate causes. One reason for the attraction of 'radicalization' as a concept after the events of 7/7 in the UK was the space it created to begin analysing and discussing the root causes in a way that was not possible before. Thus, understanding the provenance of VE through the concept of 'radicalization', despite its inherent drawbacks as a process, allowed the academic community to re-assess older problems through new a lens, which in turn allowed scholarship to push forward.

This discursive explosion of the concept of radicalization between 2005 and 2010 was inextricably linked to the demands of CT policy. However, the question of motivation has frustrated scholars for a long time. Researchers have stressed the multifaceted nature of motivations, which are difficult to identify. They are often multiple, contradictory, constantly changing with time. The objectives are not always transparent and how one thinks about and articulates them to others depends on context. Who is asking the question about motivation and whether the answers to this question are directed at a particular audience or constituency become important considerations. This has been reflected in accounts of former terrorists interviewed many years after they left terrorism behind. Some individuals and supporters of VE tend to over-emphasize the role of context, while others stress the purity of their beliefs. Outsiders examining the terrorist group tend to overstate the role of ideology, psychology and beliefs, often in pejorative terms.

Scholars have made the important distinction between 'why' and 'how' individuals become involved in terrorism. While the two questions often converge, in practice, the 'how' questions open different avenues of exploration. In academic scholarship, therefore, attention has turned to explaining the 'how' of terrorism. The 'how' questions are more about the processes and steps that individuals and groups take in their turn to VE. 'How' questions delineate the process and allow one to begin thinking about different levels of interventions. This feeds into the policy imperatives of CT. 'How' questions have also emerged from the sociological schools of social movement theory. Many of the variables present in the violent radicalization process are examined: socio-economic status, gender, psychological, religious, ideological, theological, the impact of globalization, Islamophobia, cultural, political, the role of social media/internet, meta-psychological/existential as well social movement theories and other sociological accounts. However, the most analytically rewarding theories are from social identity discourse. While scholarship into the 'how' of radicalization has made significant contributions, considerable research already existed in the pre-9/11 world. The dominance of social identity and social movement theory is a testament to the authority of older theories. Perhaps more important is the fact that even 'how' questions, while undoubtedly important in informing the formulation of policy and programmes, cannot be operationalized easily. The role of identity (belonging), the quest for significance (status) and the need for meaning are common drivers at the individual level in many contexts, but it is not obvious what can be done with such existential, personal and non-material driving forces.

Since the London attacks in 2005, policymakers, academics and public discourse have all discussed at length the causes behind 'homegrown' domestic terrorism. As noted above, addressing the 'root causes' of terrorism was disdained because it could be perceived to be legitimizing VE.[1] But what used to be an argument more associated with the left – that contexts, structure and policies matter – has become a central aspect of the CVE space. This took a few years to surface more explicitly, becoming more prominent with the emergence of the Islamic State in 2014. There was always a trend within scholarship that stressed contextual factors contributing to VE, but between 2005 and 2013, the hegemonic discourse focused on ideology, religion and identity, whilst sections of the political left and Muslim communities highlighted political reasons and Western foreign policies. The discourse today is a lot more nuanced and recent studies have significantly improved understandings of Jihadist terrorism. However, while much is known today about the factors of VE and the recalibration of CT towards addressing 'drivers', 'factors' and 'root causes', all of which are welcome achievements, a deep problem nevertheless remains with epistemology, methodology, commonly used frameworks, expertise gaps and the emergence of cottage industries with ready-packaged solutions to research and policy problems.

The problem with current frameworks

Current frameworks and typologies employed to discern the factors the lead to VE do not help to resolve why it is that only a minority of individuals engage in such a high-risk activity. The most widely used radicalization framework is 'push–pull'. *Push* factors are identified as structural or environmental conditions that can create grievances, prompting individuals to support or turn to VE. *Pull* factors are those that make violent extremist ideas and groups appealing as external factors in violence.[2] The UN CVE Plan of Action lists structural factors such as a lack of socio-economic opportunities, marginalization and discrimination, poor governance, violations of human rights and the rule of law, prolonged and unresolved conflicts and prisons. Examples of pull factors include a sense of purpose, adventure, belonging, acceptance, status, material enticement and religious incentives, such as rewards in the afterlife.³ This framework is a useful starting point in helping to conceptualize factors that may cause individuals to turn to VE; however, it remains descriptive and simplistic. It informs little about how individuals turn to political violence. Given that the framework seeks to generate multiple factors in explaining radicalization, it is difficult to isolate the critical factors that cause an individual to turn to political violence. The challenge is to establish when and why some drivers are more important than others, and which combinations are more potent than others. Although 'push' factors provide an important contextual backdrop, they do not explain the turn to political violence. For example, factors like poverty, unemployment, corruption and repressive government are widespread and affect many millions and yet only a small minority of individuals resort to VE. Many of the factors purported to drive 'pull' factors, such as belonging and ideology are in fact factors that govern the actions of all affected by them.

Although likely to capture some truth, such frameworks are nevertheless abstract and regularly de-particularized. Technical P/CVE experts start from scratch in every country, where categorizations such as 'developed' and 'developing' mean that many countries seem equivalent with regard to their VE levels. Yet, if one aims to examine the far-right, for example, such categories as 'developed' or 'Western' homogenize otherwise-diverse countries such as the United Kingdom, the United States, France and Germany. For any Western country, for bureaucrats who are often isolated from ordinary people on the ground in the places they seek to understand, communities and individuals become something entirely theoretical, a textbook reference. The P/CVE donor, or government official, feels entitled to deal with 'at-risk' and 'vulnerable' populations, which are constructs that have been created. Western governments, vis-à-vis their populations, can take the same approach. They see communities and individuals through the prism of a singular homogenized 'community', ignoring the complex histories and sets of local issues confronting local areas. Such blank-state approaches create one-size-fits-all fixes that are applied widely instead of having to study the historicity of each situation. It introduces indolence, combined with essentialism and reductionism. The alternative would be to learn from the history of each country and city/town. But CVE frameworks and typologies encourage bureaucrats, policymakers, civil society and organizations operating in the field to analyse the conditions that generate political violence in ahistorical ways. The problem with this approach is that such analyses take place long after the recruitment of individuals or after attacks – and when the situation, context and environment have all evolved. It is little wonder, then, that CVE practitioners become convinced that they know what is best for populations 'out there', far away from their desks in comfortable offices, who are deemed to be 'at-risk' and 'vulnerable', only then to determine that they still have knowledge gaps.

Despite attempts to be comprehensive in coverage, such frameworks are limited by the fact that they are static and represent little more than a picture frozen in time. Yet in the real world, many things are not static. Individuals change, evolve, groups come and go. There is a difference between the *static* and the *dynamic*. Such an analysis of the factors of VE provides a snapshot view of the complex reality on the ground; it does not reflect what happens temporally as people, groups and events change. For example, more than sixteen Sudanese medical students from the University of Medical Sciences and Technology in Sudan were recruited to join the Islamic State in 2014.[4] Sudan has chronic structural problems, including armed conflict, repression and corruption, none of which ostensibly played a role in mobilizing these medical students to join the Islamic State. Despite the permanence and persistence of many of the indicators believed to drive conflict in Sudan, it has virtually little or no VE problems. But as a state-sponsor of terrorism in the 1990s, this was not always the case. This example demonstrates that a static view of the situation, which prevalent CVE frameworks enable, cannot capture the dynamically evolving situation on the ground.

The human and social world is already too complex to understand comprehensively, not to mention the difficulty of trying to regulate human behaviour. Experts and use rational theory but their models are incoherent because they imply that the same laws do not govern these social scientists. This view of free and rational experts is incompatible with their theories of human behaviour. First, it seeks to determine the causes that trigger behaviour instead of investigating the goals that agents pursue through their choices and actions. Second, the standpoint of behaviour denies human freedom, starting from the position of determinism. These frameworks and typologies assert some order, coherence and intelligibility onto a reality governed by randomness, misfortunes and contingencies. Missing from such frameworks and the discourse in CVE more generally is an account of the role of complexity and chance in pathways to VE. In some contexts, individuals find themselves coerced into VE – a situation beyond them to control. Countries where most terrorism takes place, such as Iraq, Afghanistan, Syria, Somalia and Nigeria, are also places of armed conflict, civil war and insurgencies, and where governance is weak or has collapsed. Many individuals in these places are drawn into violence and terrorism by being in the wrong place at the wrong time, or they are inveigled into groups as a matter of survival or to avenge the loss of a loved one. Most CVE 'experts', academics and practitioners overestimate causality and tend to view the world as more explicable than it is. Outcomes relating to VE are the result of many factors, including non-random as well as random events. Yet they are presented as purely non-random.

The 'where' of recruitment to VE

There is a difference between potential and actual VE, with the success of political violence movements being determined by how well they can mobilize people and channel grievance into concrete action. Scholarship on radicalization and VE has shown that the most significant explanation for VE is found in the interaction between individuals and the group. However, even this relationship is misunderstood, largely due to an insufficient understanding of other crucial concepts used in tandem, such as 'vulnerability', as well as misdirected thinking, that is, a static rather than a dynamic view of how processes work.

Radicalization is a metaphor that emerged after 2004 in media and political circles to describe the process before the 'bomb went off'.[5] However, the concept did not emanate within academic studies and had no scientific or methodological basis, despite its currency in public discourse. Radicalization is a source of confusion, being used to understand several policy agendas (security, integration, social and political activism or even Islamist politics in the Middle East). Conceptually, however, there are three primary problems: the synonymy of radicalization with violence; how it posits a linear process from one state to another, contradicting the real-life processes individuals take; and the distinction between cognitive and behavioural factors, with the assumption that violence begins with the ideas and beliefs of individuals. While radicalization can be employed with some caveats and qualifications, one is dealing with a socialization process no different from what occurs in the army, sports teams and as a broader social experience.

The concept of radicalization fails to account for the fact that individuals join VE groups and movements for a myriad of different, often non-ideological, reasons. People align themselves with VE organizations for emotional, pragmatic, rational or opportunistic considerations. Moreover, there are two important considerations to bear in mind in how individuals turn to political violence. First, the importance of viewing terrorism in terms of a set of sequences and events building up to an attack, which is precluded from the concept of radicalization and which is better encapsulated by the concept of mobilization. Second, the need to view involvement in terrorism as a nonlinear process, often involving multiple roles and transitions over time concerning particular social groups. Here, the concept of 'recruitment' is more appropriate. Mobilization is the 'process by which radicalised individuals shift from extremist intent to preparatory steps to engage in any terrorist activity such as an attack, travel for extremist purposes or facilitating the terrorist activity of someone else'.[6] In contrast to radicalization, the concept of mobilization is more concerned with the build-up leading to an attack. For example, the Canadian Intelligence Service cites changes to the individual's physical training routine, purchasing attack preparation paraphernalia on a credit card or putting personal belongings up for sale to raise money for the intended activity as indicators of mobilization.[7] Mobilization consists of a notable shift in the pattern of behaviour that a person exhibits in their daily life. Thus, an important aspect of mobilizing to VE is the need to understand the sequences of stages and events. The following terrorist threat assessments conceptualize the preparatory conduct of terrorists as consisting of seven distinct phases.[8] Namely,

1. Ideological development
2. Personal characteristics
3. Organizational development
4. Attack planning
5. Concealment and operational security
6. Attack preparation
7. Related activities

The aims of de radicalization in CVE has been at stages 1–3. The CVE field does not pay sufficient attention to recruitment and mobilization to VE, stages 1–7. Until now, the emphasis has been on trying to prevent people from becoming terrorists rather than preventing terrorist attacks from happening, with the assumption being that in some instances ideological development and personal characteristics are sufficient to cause a turn to VE. In other words, intention to commit violence has been the barometer to gauge threat, ignoring the importance of capability in being able to undertake acts of terrorism, which is enhanced in the context of organizations, groups and during the attack preparation phase. The difference, however, between pre-attack (intention), attack preparation and attack execution (capability) is significant given that an individual radicalizing does not mean they will mobilize for an attack. It is not enough to have extreme or radical ideas, but the meaningful difference in practice is whether an individual is involved in attack preparation and execution.

Critical to involvement and engagement with terrorism is an individual's experience with organizations or groups and their exposure to radicalizing settings. Recruitment is commonly described as the ways and methods through which organizations seek to gain members or active supporters. Recruitment acknowledges the presence of an external influence drawing individuals into VE, whereas the term 'radicalization' assumes that the individual develops extreme views almost in isolation before searching out terrorist groups.[9] Recruitment to VE is normally associated with top-down methods. However, scholarship has shown that since 2004 the process of VE has been primarily bottom-up, with individuals seeking opportunities to be recruited rather than being brainwashed or manipulated into VE.[10] Within this broader understanding, therefore, the concept of 'radicalization' can be subsumed under the more analytically useful concept of 'recruitment', which can be understood to mean the process through which individuals join entities engaged in VE.[11]

The role of socialization in mobilization

Research in CVE is conducted on the drivers of VE for programming and identifying an 'at-risk' and 'vulnerable' population to prevent the next generation of terrorists from emerging. However, the sheer psychological and sociological diversity of VE militants, coupled with both the individualized and context-specific nature of pathways towards violence renders generic attempts to identify vulnerable populations as potentially ineffective and counter-productive. Furthermore, it assumes that there is a spectrum of populations, with 'vulnerable' on one end and radicalized on the other. On the vulnerable side, individuals and communities are depicted as weak and susceptible to ideological manipulation. On the one hand, they supposedly need care and lack agency. Yet on the other, they are said to pose a potential danger. First, there is no conclusive evidence regarding what makes individuals vulnerable to terrorism. Second, not all individuals are equally at risk. While some youth are indeed vulnerable, and a minority are dangerous, this understanding of the individual as vulnerable is misleading and does not reflect what is happening on the ground and in real life. For example, over 40,000 young people joined the Islamic State from over 100 countries, including over 4,000 European-born Muslims. It was the biggest counter-culture youth movement in the world. 'Vulnerability' does not fully explain this phenomenon. Third, in CVE, the general personal vulnerabilities some individuals may have are sometimes conflated with vulnerability to radicalization. A distinction must be made such that individuals vulnerable to 'radicalization' may include 'vulnerable individuals', but it remains to be demonstrated that 'vulnerable individuals' are necessarily 'vulnerable to radicalization'.

Here, insight from situational action theory is illuminating. 'Vulnerability to radicalization' does not function in the real world in terms of its presence or absence in an individual. In other words, 'vulnerability to radicalization' or becoming 'at-risk to radicalization' is not an inherent attribute within individuals or particular groups. Instead, it is a social process of varying gradation that becomes activated with 'exposure' to a radicalizing setting. Viewed in this way, vulnerability to radicalization is expressed in response to a specific situation. Some individuals indeed have a greater propensity to become radicalized to violence due to personal temperaments, biographies, moral control and idiosyncrasies. However, these susceptibility characteristics, for want of a better phrase can be expressed and manifested in a multitude of ways unrelated to terrorism. The difference is whether the individual becomes exposed to a VE setting and if they become entangled in places of recruitment and among recruiting agents. Vulnerability is best thought of as situational, not individual.

All humans are susceptible or at-risk of contracting a tropical infection known as leptospirosis, which is caught from the urine of animals. But most would not take precautions against catching it because they implicitly assess that they would not be exposed to animal urine. After all, most people have not had much exposure to places where there is soil or freshwater. It is rare to get it from people, pets or bites. It must be caught through the mouth, eyes and cuts. One may, of course, increase susceptibility to catching it if one had cuts not bandaged or covered, or did not have a supply of freshwater to drink from. But unless one has been exposed through contact in the right settings, leptospirosis cannot be caught. Individuals are only vulnerable and at risk of catching leptospirosis if they become exposed to the right setting. However, exposure to radicalizing settings varies according to individuals, times and places. Radical settings, in other words where recruitment takes place, are determined by what situational action theory defines as 'social selection' and 'self-selection'. Self-selection refers to rules and social forces that encourage, compel, discourage or bar certain people from taking part in particular kinds of time- and place-based activities. At the individual level, this social selection is a matter of the groups to which an individual belongs (e.g. ethnic, social and religious), which broadly constrain the settings an individual is likely to find themselves in. Self-selection refers to the preference-based choices people make to attend particular time- or place-based activities within the constraints of the forces of social selection. At the individual level, self-selection operates based on the preferences (likes and dislikes) a person has acquired through life experience.[12]

Exposure to radical settings, which is determined by social and self-selection, is the likely explanation as to why there does not exist a consistent profile of terrorists. The implication of this technical point about selection is significant: the profiles of individuals who become involved in terrorism are so diverse and constantly in flux because radicalization hubs or settings vary according to time, place and context. The setting, the 'where' of recruitment and radicalization, is determined by the social group a person belongs to and the place a person likes to go or avoids. The role of social selection is reflected by the fact affective bonds of friendship and kinship are crucial in pulling people into the orbit of VE. These trends frame the membership of the Islamic State, where 95 per cent of foreign fighters joined through familial or peer networks.[13] Research in the 1980s on VE groups in Italy and Germany demonstrated that friendship ties go deeper than radical political or religious propositions; creating a sense of in-group connection and identity that intensifies when threatened by external agencies.[14] Moreover, there are national differences in recruiting patterns. Recruits in the UK, for example, are drawn predominantly from citizens of Pakistani and Caribbean origin, with Pakistan serving as the main place of training. In France and Belgium, recruits hail from North and West African backgrounds and they have been more successful than their British counterparts in getting to Arabic-speaking Iraq for training. Recruits in Northern Europe have been dominated by second- and third-generation citizens with an immigrant background, whereas recruitment in Southern European countries like Spain and Italy occurs among the first generation of migrants from the Arabic-speaking world.

In practice, social and self-selection settings are interlinked. In the context of Jihadist VE, examples of recruitment settings have included prisons, universities, mosques, gyms, halal restaurants and private spaces because these settings are where Muslims meet and congregate and where, due to higher degrees of vigilance by the authorities, recruitment has been driven underground. Equally significant is how particular settings may convert the latent propensity among certain individuals because they constitute places of heightened uncertainty. In places such as prisons, universities and more recently among migrants (migration being an experience in which people find themselves in new and chaotic places), VE recruiters take advantage of the lack of orientation and personal crisis that some young people have. Furthermore, the internet has come to play an increasingly important role in VE recruitment, either in support of 'real-world' recruitment or in entirely new militant activism described as 'virtual self-recruitment'. However, it is the affordance of the internet, how it encourages certain behaviours and makes certain activities possible that connects a person to new preferences with other types of social selections.

In this chapter, alternative models of how we should articulate a framework for understanding the turn to political violence argue that its study has to be inter-disciplinary. It needs to bring together science (humans as biological), social science (psychology, politics and sociology) and the humanities (philosophy, history, religion and culture). It has to place the question of 'why' back into the analysis of political violence, emphasizing the importance of history, politics and context. Indeed, there are numerous situational drivers of terrorism to consider, including political, economic and social grievances; personal factors (e.g. the desire to avenge a loved one); material incentive (the search for economic gain); much broader ideological (especially religious) objectives; and intimidation or coercion by peers or the community. This classification tries to answer the 'why' question regarding an individual incentive for joining a violent group. These are not exhaustive and nor do they reflect the complexity involved in variables as subjective and elusive as 'motivations' in the real world; in fact, such motivations often overlap, override and change over time for individuals. Based on the literature, however, they present a simple but useful schematic for the reasons individuals become terroristic. Additional caution must be taken about this literature because it primarily focuses on Muslim diasporas in the West (albeit some of it draws on older terrorism literature), which may reduce its transferability to another context, in particular in the global south. The following chapter aims to further disentangle the reasons why terrorism occurs.

6

The social science of extremism

After exploring the dominant overarching *push* and *pull* approaches to understanding the processes of radicalization in the previous chapter, the focus now is to distinguish between domestic and external grievances. General examples of domestic grievances include the reality and the perception of being discriminated against in the labour market, a lack of opportunities and anomie. This feeling of marginalization and alienation becomes acute when individuals perceive that their failure to succeed socially and economically is because they are 'different' racially, ethnically and religiously from the dominant group in society. Social and economic problems then attain a political significance, often creating political protest movements that aim to rectify existing historical injustices or structural inequalities experienced by the marginalized group. Indeed, in the global south, this tends to be the primary factor. External grievances refer to events in the world, foreign policy and war, and perceptions of injustice in international affairs. This, '[u]sually entails the perception that the West and/or the US are fundamentally hostile to Islam and Muslim.'[1] In the context of Western Europe, external grievance often means the perception that the West is at war with Islam, where the spark of radicalization occurs in the Western context when both domestic and external grievances are aligned.[2] Such a reality is entirely consistent with the impact of the *push* factors seen in cases of VE more generally, but their interaction with *pull* factors remains necessary in order to be activated into violence. The nexus is at the level of the individual – and this is why it is only possible to understand radicalization at this level of analysis.

Contrary to rational choice theory and utilitarian models of cost–benefit analysis, human beings are meaning-seeking creatures. It is sacred values that people are willing to die for, and not just Islam or religious fanaticism, and sacred values are not up for sale.[3] This in part explains the consternation of many liberals, who view humans as rational social animals seeking their self-interest. Those with sacred values sacrifice their self-interest and life for the sake of the group and the defence of sacred values, something that also puzzles Darwinists and evolutionists. This is why individuals have died for not just religion but also the tribe, the nation, the environment, animals, freedom, communism and so on. Religion does not have a monopoly on sacred values and nor is it the sole instigator of violence. In a study of over 2,000 foreign fighters in Al Qaeda-linked movements, the observation was that 'they all were looking for something […] they want to understand who they are, why they matter, and what their role in the world should be. They have an unfulfilled need to define themselves, which al-Qaida offers to fill'.[4]

Personal grievances

A high proportion of young people are drawn to VE because of their need to belong to a group for the purposes of self-validation and a sense of excitement. Social alienation caused by daily boredom, unemployment, lack of status and a deep sense of pessimism regarding prospects can make joining violent extremist groups a rewarding incentive. There is substantial research, especially in psychology, showing that identity at the individual level – how an individual sees or describes him or herself – is highly significant in drawing individuals towards terrorism.[5] This theory provides a sophisticated psychological model of the terrorist 'mindset' and 'worldview' that combines vulnerabilities, such as the search for identity, with propensities. A young person in search of identity who has a strong predisposition to identifying external threats may be at a much higher risk than someone whose identity has formed and who lacks those propensities. It is difficult to measure the extent to which this potential instability affects different people, but such sustained turmoil could create a 'cognitive opening' or a personal crisis in just the same way as a violent or traumatic event could. First, the state of uncertainty is considered a 'threat to life': when individuals feel uncertain, they look for groups with cohesive and clear guidelines and are more likely to adopt and adhere to delineated, and often polarizing norms. Second, it can help explain how this uncertainty can make individuals vulnerable to the lure of extremist groups.

Useful here too is the concept of 'ontological security', which is the idea of a stable mental state derived from a sense of continuity concerning events in an individual's life.[6] This is reliant on people's ability to give meaning to their lives, which is found when experiencing positive and stable emotions, and by avoiding chaos and anxiety. Ontological security involves having a positive view of *self*, the world and the future. The group, following social movement theory, therefore, is why the individual experiences 'ontological security'. These groups provide them with the opportunity to experience a sense of sacrifice and in-group honour. In some cases, it provides them with combat skills as well as adrenaline-inducing tasks. Moreover, once young recruits become socialized into the narratives of extremist groups, the identity of the individual is fused with the identity of the group. This means that the individual feels a moral duty to defend and advance the group's interest, which is perceived to be aligned with the interest of the individual.[7] From a religious perspective, many violent extremists are seeking a sense of spiritual purification through armed struggle and a sense of purification for past sins (many are 'born again' Salafis), and are operating on the battlefield under the belief that they will be rewarded in heaven for their actions on earth. The organization provides an identity, while meeting other needs, such that 'in radical movements and extremist groups, many prospective terrorists find not only a sense of meaning but also a sense of belonging, connectedness and affiliation'.[8] This is why 'radicalization' itself is often regarded as a 'social process', not an ideological one.

The role of status is vital in understanding individual incentives to engage in VE. One aspect of status is linked to the concept of 'recognition'.[9] Theories of recognition state that all humans desire and need social validation and recognition from others and society. This 'recognition' represents a form of self-actualization.[10] The striking feature of status and recognition today is the proliferation of other ways of attaining recognition. As a result of the internet (especially social media) and cultural and social transformation in the last two decades, instead of aspiring to move up the conventional social hierarchy, in this new environment, millennials seek status in alternative ways. Rather than having to operate in a dominant social hierarchy, one can attain status by belonging to a niche group with its internal values. It is, therefore, possible to gain status by belonging to a group – 'I'm a vegetarian hipster', 'I'm a liberal environmentalist' or 'I'm a Jihadi Muslim'. Further status is gained by demonstrating excellence in the traits essential to the group. In the case of neo-Jihadi groups, this entails external conformity to dress and behavioural codes and the willingness, in some cases, to sacrifice the self for the cause. Youths join violent groups for recognition and status among a small band of brothers brought together under a common cause.

Material inducements

Many individuals are motivated to join violent groups for material gains. There are also links between young militants living a life of petty crime in Western cities and joining the Islamic State. For example, in resource-poor environments, leaders attract recruits by drawing on social ties to make credible promises about the private rewards that come with victory.[11] Joiners stay away from these movements, leaving a pool of compliant recruits willing to invest their time and energy in the hope of reaping large gains in the future.

A theory that takes individuals as rational actors and articulates the importance of expectation is the 'rising frustration' thesis.[12] This notes that relative deprivation is essentially the discrepancy between what is called *value expectancies* (what individuals expect) and *value expectations* (what they receive). When the gap between what individuals expect and what they get grows too large, they are likely to become discontented and mobilize politically. However, people are most inclined to rebel when they perceive inequity in the wretchedness of their condition. People recognize that deprivation exists, but when they become aware that their deprivation is not universal – that is, they are relatively more deprived than others – they develop a perspective that their deprivation is unfair and realize the necessity of political action to change their conditions. For many young men and women, frustrations occur due to the expectation of individuals and the failure to actualize their needs or wants, which are subsequently met in violent groups.

In the global south, an example of material needs includes getting married in the MENA region, a prospect unthinkable without the assistance of others because it is often beyond the economic means of most young people to get married and start a family. There is evidence suggesting that some organizations, including the Islamic State, provided a salary for violent extremists, as well as offering money and support to their families. While it is true that material wants and needs are provided by violent groups, individuals may also be driven by ideological fervour and/or by religious convictions. The relative importance of 'grievance' and 'ideology' may vary depending on whether one is focusing on leaders or rank-and-file members. However, ideology has a goal, enemies, a worldview, an internal and external audience and a strategy for realizing its goal. As a rule, ideology's primary role may not be to attract individuals to VE organizations, but in the wake of intense social interaction it can help to deepen and solidify individual commitments to those organizations. Violent extremist groups may force communities to provide them with passive or active support or even recruits. Coercion is likely to be a salient factor in areas where the government lacks a substantial presence and cannot provide security and protection to its citizens, in particular in the global south. It is crucial to note that these outcomes are not abstractions from 'ideology'. They are genuine intellectual and moral attempts by people to identify with an imagined community and who share an identity, history and a common future.

Whilst there would appear to be material benefits in joining violent or extremist organizations, in reality, however, there are limitations. The spoils of war are often shared unequally, with commanders and senior operators benefiting far more disproportionately than the average foot soldier. Rather, in some cases, there are no material benefits to be gained from associations within the context of a struggle or conflict. In reality, many who join the ranks of extremist organizations 'offer the optimal combination of effectiveness and ease of retention'.[13]

Salafi-Jihadism

It is the broader umbrella concept of cultural re-birth that acts as a master signifier suturing the vast spectrum of Islamism, from its peaceful articulations to its more violent manifestations. The cultural re-birth project of Islam is based on an intersubjective reality. It is a world with internalized narratives, history, sources of morality, values norms, legitimate authority, trends, symbols, meaning, charismatic individuals, archetypes, heroes and aspirations for the future. It is a broad 'church', which has porous boundaries and no institutions to police its orthodoxy, positions and trajectories. Hence, the problem of who speaks for Islam: everyone and nobody. Within an imagined porous community that anyone can dip into, there is always a struggle between conflicting trends, values and beliefs. A tiny minority within this broad church takes it upon itself to define the response to the challenges of modernity, globalization, the state and war, among other social, economic and cultural threats in VE terms. Jihadi political violence is a strategic response and solution to long-standing narratives that originate from a century and half of turmoil, upheaval, rapture and fragmentation. These individuals are responding to real events in their lives: those posed in their local community, in their countries and across the globe. It results from a failure of current political regimes in the Middle East, North Africa and Asia to provide and protect its people from domestic oppression and outside interference. It results from the failure to respond to the modern world with confidence, innovation and creativity with a defensive response to an imagined community that feels humiliated and insulated, yearning for dignity and self-esteem.

There are three main strands of Salafi groups: purists, politicos and Jihadis.[14] Whilst there is some overlap of beliefs, Salafi-jihadist thinking is the most problematic because it is founded on a violent programme that both feeds on and promotes violent conflict as an end in itself. This distinction between Salafism (a conservative movement with millions of followers globally) and Salafi-jihadism (a minority within the Islamist movement) is crucial because it allows the ability to focus on the primary source of contemporary VE in many parts of the world. Groups such as Al Qaeda and Islamic State belong to the Salafi-jihadi movement and describe themselves in these terms.[15] Salafi-jihadist ideology provides intellectual justification for the delegitimization of existing political institutions. It permits its adherents to identify an 'enemy' and promotes the use of violence as a religious obligation to bring an Islamic order and polity into existence. It integrates a stringent religious reform agenda with a political programme, sanctifying the role of violence in bringing both together. The question of identity is central in the journey of an individual who moves from confused, alienated and marginalized young Muslim into a violent, aggressive extremist whose motivations are driven by ideological considerations.[16] It is combined with opportunity structures through networks, where 'radicalization can be understood as a process of first fostering an increase in religious awareness and then manipulating this awareness for political ends'.[17]

In preventing VE in the global north, it is necessary to establish a firm foundation on which disaffected young Muslims in the diaspora can ascertain themselves. It is often the case that there is no bottom floor for many who face problems of social immobility and underachievement. This necessarily focuses on questions relating to economic development, social cohesion and political participation, which are often nowhere to be seen in the context of CVE policy development and practice, although, '[u]ltimately, terrorism is a moral problem with psychological underpinnings; the challenge is to prevent disaffected youth and others from becoming engaged in the morality of terrorist organizations'.[18] It is related not just to actual but also perceived levels of discrimination and marginalization. This is essential to bear in mind, given the generally toxic environment that Muslim groups in the Western European diaspora continue to face. It is the reality that often faces the tormented individual but it is also the perception of the group, thus reinforcing the need for a individuals to establish themselves in communities, and in urban cleavages where there are already existing patterns of concentrated groups in often marginalized areas.

Social psychology

Much of the emphasis in considering why an individual might carry out a terrorist attack tends to focus on individual factors, with significance given to concerns relating to mental illness, psychological disorders or personality traits. These provide some comfort in suggesting that somehow these individuals are not like us. However, scientific evidence tends to assert that most of these assailants are very much like everyone else. That is, they are exceptionally normal. Recent studies have identified three primary factors to consider in any understanding of the processes of radicalization, leading to extremism and terrorism: individual motivation (needs), ideological justification (narratives) and group processes (networks).[19] Here, radicalized groups share characteristics with gangs, including within prisons.[20]

Criminologists, sociologists and psychologists often concentrate on the notion of humiliation and how individuals seek to redress the imbalance created by it through carrying out acts that redeem the loss of status or self-worth. This is channelled through ideology for it is considered as a primary opportunity structure – a space through which to retrieve the loss of status. As an external enemy is determined, the justification for violence towards it is rationalized, with indoctrination acting as the final step, which 'frees adherents of the ideology to act violently without the burden of guilt typically attached to perpetration of violence'.[21] In mobilizing this dehumanization into violence and aggression, networks are necessary, as without them there would be far greater instances of violence among existing angry, disenfranchised and alienated young Muslims throughout Europe, who all face various concerns concerning the loss of status as a result of marginalization, racism and Islamophobia. In this regard, networks are seen as the second foremost opportunity structure after ideology. Individuals are not drawn to radical Islam on their own. They do so in groups of similar like-minded individuals, with group concentration acting to further substantiate values, attitudes and sentiments that can lead to violence and terrorism. The group justifies the Individual. By understanding these 'needs, narratives and networks', a clearer picture of radicalization emerges.[22]

There are Numerous instances of individuals who have left organizations such as the Islamic State because they did not fulfil their initial expectations. With these concerns in mind, it is conceivable to reverse engineer these processes, thus leading to notions of deradicalization. In some cases individuals have returned to their sending countries upon arrival. There are instances of individuals who became disillusioned by the ideological perspectives of the group, and thus contributing to their reversion. Many abandoned the Islamic State because of the infighting. Some deserted because other Muslims were seen as legitimate targets within the ideological perspective of the group. This is compounded with disillusionment over the leaders of the group, which discourages individuals to maintain the fight for what they thought was the cause.

The quest for significance, therefore, remains a critical matter in understanding the social-psychological dimensions of radicalization. But the role of social networks is critical in ascertaining the activation that an individual undergoes. A combination of feelings of insignificance at an individual level is enhanced within the network, including among friends and family members, who can reinforce their original perspectives. The importance of social influence, therefore, is considerable.[23]

Space and Place

The role of space has hitherto been largely neglected by scholars. The influence space on matters such as the formation communities, identities and other dynamics develop has been marginalized in accounts of VE. The advent of space as a unit of analysis in the social sciences originated with the works of Henry Lefebvre and his concept of the 'social production of space'.[24] It questioned deep assumptions about the material construction of space, illustrating the socially constructed nature of how space develops. Material reality, consequently, is not just 'there', but is contingent upon a whole range of interconnected factors such as how it is imagined, conceived and ordered around such elements such like language. Another dimension to the role of space is presented by the concept of 'heterotopia',[25] which describes spaces that have greater layers of meaning or relationships to other places than immediately meet the eye. A heterotopia is a physical representation or approximation of a utopia or a parallel space (such as a prison, hospital or school) that contains undesirable bodies to make a utopian space realizable. This insight on the construction of structures and spaces to remove undesirable bodies and to make room for more congruent bodies is helpful in understanding how local areas develop and with it how certain populations. A striking representation of this concept is physically embodied in the cities of Paris, Birmingham or Lyon in the way that immigrant and diaspora communities are positioned outside and around the city, resembling a ring. This material arrangement of bodies impacts on how individuals and communities perceive themselves, others, and their place within their respective localities. It underlines the significant role space has in the formation of urban and rural communities and the phenomenological experience it induces.

A main feature of the spatial formations evident in urban cities is the role of economic opportunities, not only in acting as a 'pull' factor in migration patterns but also their impact on socio-cultural trends. Given that major urban cities in Europe such as London, Paris and Berlin are attractive locations for employment and thus prime sites for the embedding of plural and diverse communities, what then is the impact of urban geographical space formation on how diaspora ethnic communities compete for resources? What is the impact of structural transformations on communities shifting away from traditional industries such as manufacturing and coal mining to service and finance based economics? As both far-right and Islamist extremisms often emerge locally due to narrow definitions of citizenship, belonging and nationhood,[26] space and place can compound existing exclusionary discourses on differences based on ethnicity, religious identity, socio-economic status and politics. In local urban areas, deep-rooted contestations can exist over the struggle for hegemony based on a hyper-imagined 'them' and 'us', revealing urban spatial formations against the backdrop of the global-local nexus of ethnic nationalism and widening social divisions in Western Europe. How these factors affect radicalization within certain localities is less well understood because few studies investigate the synergies between the far-right and Muslim extremists, two seemingly parallel experiences, in a comparative context.[27]

Equally significant to the flourishing of diaspora migrant communities is the development and creation of sites of cultural repertoire. The performativity of culture, religion and identity, which is crucial for the acculturalization of individuals and communities into norms and practices of their culture, is contingent in part on the site of performances: the mosque, the shisha café, the home. One way of looking at the development of cultural identity, then, is that identities are the regular performance of normative patterns and paradigms and places and sites, which become personalized locations charged with emotional and cultural signification in which gender, ethnic, racial and class norms are performed. Aside from the physical component, there is an imaginative dimension to the spatial formation. The ideational function of space is dependent on how one construes and discursively frames phyiscal spaces. An instructive concept to discuss here is 'community', which has become a hackneyed term in popular discourse and policymaking circles. However, the notion of community has shifted once more from the nation, amongst second and third-generation European diaspora, to someplace else, the imagined community of the faithful or the 'Ummah'. It has become a global transcultural imaginary utopia, where the Ummah and specifically the Caliphate, can mobilize thousands of Muslims globally, with sympathy evident across the globe. Here, Islamism is comparable to nationalism, which is a response to the loss of identity and mass-level spiritual Islam because of the movement from rural to urban areas, alienation and loss of meaning. The power of imaginative spaces to reconstruct communities and identities is particularly acute in instances of modernization and urbanization. Questions relating to the discussions of the urban sphere are developing further in the following chapter.

7

Reciprocal radicalization

There are individual, situational and psychological factors to take into account when attempting to understand the nature of extremism among individuals motivated by needs, narratives and networks that can be mobilized into VE. Among the factors to consider are the issues of political context, and how it can motivate radicalized youth to seek opposing narratives in the relation to the 'other', even when this 'other' is a mirror to the 'self'. As the reality of right-wing populism and ethnic nationalism takes an ever-greater hold, there is a growing problem of a general yet persistent move to the right in mainstream politics in contemporary Europe.[1] This is the case not only in developed Western democracies such as the UK, Germany and the Netherlands but also in newer liberal states such as Poland, Hungary and Slovakia. The end of the Cold War is a useful starting point for understanding this development. Here, the long-standing post-war order changed irrevocably, leading to a period of centrist politics between the fall of the Berlin Wall and the start of the 'war on terror' over a decade later. From the grassroots of these societies, a range of social movements emerged – including fascist groups that carried out an 'ideological facelift' in the 1990s,[2] with each successively problematizing the issues of Muslims. Until recently, the electoral successes of the right have been negligible – leading to a sense of political disenchantment. This was the case until the Brexit vote in the UK, which was partly motivated by negative discourses on immigration, refugees and questions of national political identity.[3]

Far-right and Islamophobic attacks which result in Islamist-inspired terrorism reflect a shift within broader right-wing extremism, with many groups and individuals condemning Nazism, fascism and anti-Semitism but defining their cause as a defence against the perceived threat from Islam.[4] Anders Breivik, the Norwegian terrorist responsible for the Utøya island attacks and the bombing of the Regjeringskvartalet quarter in Oslo, outlined his disregard for 'multicultural hell'. A significant proportion of 'lone actor' terrorists, however, are solely preoccupied with neo-Nazi symbolism and the idolization of far-right figureheads and their ideologies. Until recently, there has been relative underreporting and under-analysis of the threat from right-wing extremism in North America and Europe.[5] In the case of the March 2019 attack in Christchurch, New Zealand, Brenton Tarrant a self-identified white supremacist, who viewed the world in Manichean terms, regarding Islam and Muslims as a movement and its people that deserve to be depopulated because they present a risk to the survival of the 'white nation' itself. However, there is no perspective on the nature of this whiteness; that is, its internal diversity or the historical legacies of class formation, colonialism, orientalism, eugenics or white nationalism that have defined the space occupied by whiteness, all of which seemingly legitimizing ethnic nationalism and white supremacism.

It is now increasingly apparent that an anti-Muslim outlook plays a part in radicalizing far-right extremists, reflecting on the notion of 'reactive co-radicalization'[6] or 'cumulative extremism',[7] which is considered to be a response on the parts of states, organizations, groups and individuals to the apparent threat of Muslims in the West.[8] These sentiments have become a defining feature of current Islamophobia,[9] much of which demonstrates a correlation with rising populism and nationalism. In recent years, the far right has exhibited a discernible shift from ethno-racial to cultural–ideological VE. Anders Breivik objected to various ideological strands: not merely ethnic and religious differences in society but also the ideologies and philosophies of multiculturalism and diversity underpinning them. Breivik was also hostile to broadly conceived notions such as Marxism and liberalism.[10]

As research on extremist identity politics in Western Europe is increasingly focusing on the intersection of violent radical Islamism and far-right extremism among young men, both extremisms often emerge locally due to narrow definitions of citizenship, belonging and nationhood, where space and place can compound existing exclusionary discourses on differences based on ethnicity, religious identity, socio-economic status and politics. In local urban areas, deep-rooted contestations can exist over the struggle for hegemony based on a hyper-imagined 'them' and 'us', revealing urban spatial formations against the backdrop of the global–local nexus of ethnic nationalism and widening social divisions in Western Europe. How these factors affect radicalization within particular localities is less well understood because few studies investigate the synergies between the far-right and Muslim extremists, two seemingly parallel experiences, in a comparative context.[11]

Whilst interest in radicalization has grown exponentially since the events of 9/11, much of the attention has been on Islamist extremism. But several extremisms have come to the fore in recent periods, including the idea of reciprocal radicalization when elements of the radical right specifically rally around counter-jihad sentiment. Their opposition to each other is determined by structural and cultural factors, exacerbated by local area issues of identity, space and place defined by narratives determined by the political centre of the country. The essential issue is that while both sets of groups have similar structural driving forces, there are cultural separations between them: as one is a minority, the other majority. Moreover, one group is racialized while the other racializes, but both sets of groups are at the margins of society, with their similar socio-structural realities acting as the basis for reciprocal hate, demonization and enmity. But the radical Islamists look beyond the local for a solution, as defined by their ideological bent, while the radical far right seeks to 'reclaim the local' to connect with a political discourse that is anti-Muslim, anti-immigration and anti-EU.

Unequal economic relations

Muslims who came to Britain at the end of the Second World War found themselves subordinated and subjugated by the workings of industrial capitalism. After its demise and replacement by neoliberal globalization, many of these Muslim communities were restricted to the inner city areas to which they first migrated. In the 1950s and 1960s, in locations such as Birmingham, parts of the north and areas in Greater London, diverse groups lived cheek by jowl with indigenous Britons *and* in relatively peaceful harmony. As the pace of deindustrialization accelerated, the extent of 'white flight' was enhanced due to fears of residential concentration at the hands of specific ethnic minority groups accused of fragmenting communities. In various parts of these same inner-city areas today, while those groups who desired to leave have left, minority and majority, what remains are the poorest and most excluded of white Britons. In these areas, the third- and fourth-generation Muslim minority groups are trapped due to racism, social immobility, and cultural separateness. It leads to excluded groups in society who are in intense competition for the least in society, where Islam has replaced race and ethnicity as the main categories of difference. A crucial feature in the radicalization of far-right and Islamist extremists is, therefore, the search for an alternative, 'purer' identity in response to the emergence of seemingly rival groups.[12]

Since the global financial crash of 2008, growing inequality exacerbated by the policies of austerity has led to downward social mobility for numerous indigenous majorities and Muslim minority groups, particularly in post-industrial urban localities. However, the effects of neoliberalism have a much longer historical trajectory. It has led to repercussions for youth identities, particularly in urban spheres. Men who had a rite of passage in the workplaces of factories and plants, from young person to adult, increasingly face the reality of unemployment or under-employment due to the decline of industry and manufacturing, compounded by an inability to upskill for a service sector economy. These downward social pressures exacerbate existing problems, especially in the inner cities that are sites of diverse communities. Here, residential concentration emerges largely through a lack of choice, not through choice. Post-war ethnic minorities cluster in specific urban areas to utilize social, economic and cultural capital for group survival. Simultaneously, the spatial concentration of deprived marginalized majorities is an opportunity to protect norms and values associated with the group identity, which, in the light of present politics, perceives a threat from the 'other'. The general overriding social policy discourse, however, is to present 'self-styled segregation' among Muslim minorities as a self-induced rejection of integration. This discourse, though, is harmful to many minorities who are on the receiving end of frequent vilification, alienation and discrimination. It is devoid of historical content concerning the effects of transformations to the economy and the role of housing policy during this period.[13]

Deindustrialization, post-industrialization and globalization affect Muslim minority groups in the inner cities of Britain, but these concerns also affect majority groups who can turn to far-right political views for solace.[14] Majority white communities can also suffer from these sociological predicaments that lead to extremism, radicalization and violence, but media and political discourses concentrate less on such groups, markedly skewing the debate. From 1970 to 2012, Islamist extremists carried out 2.5 per cent of all terrorist attacks in the United States compared to 4.9 per cent for Jewish groups. That is, over 90 per cent of all attacks were carried out by non-Muslims.[15] During 2016–2017, the number of attacks by far-right groups quadrupled in the United States and increased by 43 per cent in Europe.[16] The reshaping to local economies have led to a crisis of masculinity, where traditional practices of patriarchy are being challenged by the liberalization and casualization of labour markets compounded by questions of intergenerational disconnect. A crisis of masculinity (and femininity) is at the centre of many of the predicaments facing marginalized communities, underpinned by a lack of social mobility, persistent unemployment, growing anomie and political disenfranchisement, fuelling a national identity crisis, and therefore confirming a distinct relationship between gender and radicalization. The effects are anger, fear, loathing, intimidation and violence, led chiefly by the motivations of young men. Islamist radicals are anti-globalization, while far-right extremists are anti-localization, but both are pro-totalitarian. These groups wish to instil a sense of purist identity politics and both have a utopian vision of society but both also have a narrowly defined vision of the 'self', which is exclusive of the 'other'.

Masculinity challenged

In many ways, two sets of 'left behind' groups are in direct competition with each other, with both emerging in the context of neoliberalism and economic restructuring in post-industrial urban settings. As social divisions widen, these groups remain angry, voiceless and underrepresented. For far-right groups, they vehemently hold onto a sense of identity presented to them as potentially at risk due to the emergence of other groups in a society seemingly taking away or diluting the purity of this identity. Such representations are ideological, selective and political. After the events of 9/11, multiculturalism began to be seen in wholly negative terms due to the conservative politics of anti-Europeanism and ethnic nationalism that came alongside it. Being English remains closely associated with Anglo-Saxon blood. Race is the signifier here, but an imagined race, as is perennially the case when it comes to ethnic nationalism.

Part of the reason for the radicalization of both European-born Muslims and far-right youth is their coming to terms with hegemonic masculinity in the context of intergenerational disconnect, combined with economic insecurity.[17] At the level of the individual, various social, psychological, economic and structural issues can problematize the formation of identities, introducing the need for self-actualization, which is the realization of individual potential. A lack of hope leads to psychological conundrums, leaving countless young men vulnerable, exposed and then pliable to external influences. With limited educational and employment opportunities due to entrenched patterns of discrimination and disadvantage, the uncertain futures facing various young men in inner-city areas, minority and majority, create challenges with limited opportunities. Notably, these anxieties affect young men of all backgrounds, and include notions such as heterosexual, attractive and high earning. For example, Britain First, the English Defence League, and what were organizations such as Al-Muhajiroun and Islam4UK consisted largely of young men with limited education, employment or social status. These men appear to be outraged and simultaneously embittered by the spiritual or material challenges of their existence. Many of the recruits to Islamic State heralding from the inner cities of Western Europe displayed similar anxieties and aspirations.

The phenomenon of 'convert radicalization' among white groups is associated with a lack of suitable grounding in community values or the adoption of Islam as a method of rebellion.[18] Here, intergenerational disconnect and the importance of the socio-economic and socio-cultural context are important considerations in the experiences of both 'white' majorities and Muslim minorities. A broad sense of alienation transpires among a wide range of communities due to the political, religious and cultural transformations to the social milieu that have occurred in light of developments to thinking and practice on localization and globalization. Amid material challenges facing young men (and women) in Western European and North American societies, concerns arise over hyper-masculinity and hyper-sexuality (an over-concentration on sexual activity).[19] This apprehension refers to unrealistic expectations placed upon young people. It creates fear, anger and anguish, rather than a smooth transition from youth to adulthood. 'Jihadis' and far-right young men experience equivalent challenges, where differences in religion and culture regarding the 'other' are problematized and subsequently politicized. In considerable ways, hyper-masculinity diminishes the confidence of young people. The consequences are that young people become encouraged to prove themselves – to seek recognition, to become somebody – and by using any means necessary.

Both radical Islamists and far-right groups feed off the 'othering' of groups presented as oppositional to their local and global identity formations, where both groups are experiencing the fragmentation of masculinities. These have been displaced because of the shifting economic contours of post-industrial societies and the impact of deindustrialization upon traditional labour market practices as well as the withering of national identities due to neoliberal globalization. They are retreating into violent hegemony as solutions to their malaise. The response on the part of the state is often to reinforce a narrow historical reading of society and the closing down of discussions relating to diversity, inclusion and multiculturalism rather than to focus on equality, integration and social interdependence in the light of widening inequalities, a decline in political trust and increasing cultural division. Young people are susceptible to numerous challenges, but while hate crimes spike due to acts of violence after various terrorist attacks, the reality is that this loathing does not abate over time.

The end of diversity

Unquestionably, a process of the 'othering' of groups has evolved. During this time, the nation has remained consistent in its approach, although its intensification has transformed, with narratives rarely shifting away from the idea of problematic immigrants coming onto the shores of the land to exploit its resources, take advantage of its women or to subdue existing laws and ideals. This exacerbation emerges from centuries of imperialism, colonialism, eugenics and scientific racism leading to deep-seated structural and cultural racism. In the current period, the 'other' is not simply a threat based on the classical tropes of racism. It takes on a newfound purpose based on questions of national security; such are the consequences of the 'war on terror' culture that has dominated the landscape of discussions of Muslim–non-Muslim relations that have emerged since the end of the Cold War. Politicians increasingly tilting to the right focus on immigration as a way in which to protect society from 'alien others' whose alleged objectives are only to dilute and dissect. Vehemently re-expressed by groups facing downward economic and social mobility, which consequently project their anxiety outwardly, such sentiments lead to alarm and, to an extent, hate towards their nearest neighbours, namely Muslim minority groups.

The question of the associations between two sets of similar experiences points to local area considerations. The failures to introduce policies that bring about equality and fairness to limit the deleterious consequences of neoliberalism are evident. This disappointment is over the loss of the imagination of the nation in a global climate of inequality and competition, where national elites hold onto an imagined notion of the nation as well its peoples. No more are concerns over social justice and equality presented as major planks in policy thinking, but rather vacuous notions such as 'values', which has no direct purpose in bringing communities together as, in reality, these 'values' are exclusive rather than inclusive. Groups already facing downward pressures on social mobility are pushed further down by the machinations of elite groups, leading to intense levels of competition and conflict in certain local area communities, in some cases reaching fever pitch, violence and, in many cases, terrorism. Thus, both sets of VE are the result of the biopolitics of the state, but among groups in opposition to each other due to narrow definitions of identity.[20]

These realities emerge in various spatial formations, reflecting the search for self-actualization due to their 'left behind' status with few or no alternative routes to granting empowerment or status concerning the 'self'. The impact of structural and cultural determinants is leading to divergent group mobilizations, with far-right groups aiming to 'get their country back' based on claims to local-area social geographies and the apparent risks posed by diversity and multiculturalism. Simultaneously, due to historical and ongoing patterns of withdrawal, alienation and marginalization, Islamists are alluding to global identities that affirm supra-national bonds that appeal because of their politico-ideological associations with an absolutist utopian vision. As the levels of frustration among certain young Muslim men lead to the point of no return, they vent their anger at the global level, rendering their local area realities invisible. Many Muslim men do not fight for their local communities, but for an imagined global project, leading to a further vacuum at the local level, filled by the manoeuvrings of right-wing politics, fermented locally but curated nationally and internationally.

As rival tribes emerge, radicalized groups determine a core narrative at the heart of their newfound tribalistic radicalization.[21] Membership of this new menagerie is both ascriptive and aspirational, shaped by how young people use the internet as an instrument in their radicalization.[22] This lack of clarity over what radicalization is distorts the understandings of VE, in particular where there is confusion over clearly problematic social outcomes that are high-priority security threats. No two countries define 'radicalization' in the same way. For some, violence is the main concern. For others, an ideology that may or may not lead to violence is the primary focus. All definitions, nevertheless, recognize the notion as a highly individualized and largely unpredictable process.[23] Radicalization is a problematic concept, with myriad elements vital in determining the nature of the radicalized when the removal of certain variables has an overarching effect, but in other cases, a single trigger is a reason for the tipping point to radicalization, which remains an obscure and undefined compound variable. Moreover, radicalization does not always equate with terrorism.[24]

A 'war on terror' culture

Since the events of 9/11 and further terrorist incidents in Western Europe, Muslim groups have been objectified and vilified, routinely regarded as the most visible 'other' based on intensification of existing stereotypes and generalizations. Muslim groups are frequently accused of problematic behaviours such as 'grooming', subjugating women or supporting Islamist terrorism en masse. They are presented as the 'enemy within', increasingly thought to be susceptible to radicalization and VE. Muslims are regarded as risks to society, where Islam is presented as a parallel legal and social code. At the same time, legislation against terrorism invariably centres on Muslim groups, perpetuating the view that they are legitimate targets for CT policies.[25] Similarly, supporters of far-right political agendas founded on ethno-religious uniformity face recriminations based on historical associations with fascism and racism. The targeting of both Muslims and supporters of the far-right agenda has intensified the likelihood of the bipolar radicalization of ideas and attitudes.

Discussion on radicalization cannot generate new ideas without greater consideration of the social and economic contexts in which it occurs. If groups pitted against each other are in a state of perennial conflict, the conclusion is to focus on the actions of the dominant towards the dominated, with the idea of challenging the power, authority and hegemony of those who seek to subjugate the 'other' or the minority. These categories are central in determining individual behaviour at the level of communities, where individuals outside of their immediate communities are moved to extremism, radicalization and in some cases, terrorism as a response to those very communities but also to aspects of society. It is, therefore, crucial to be careful in relying on narrow theories or emotional responses to this malaise. Arguably, this has been part of the problem for too long. In understanding local area concerns affecting the urban spatial formations of bio-extremisms, the local and global intersect at the point at which groups are furthest apart culturally, socially and politically but closest together in terms of their socio-economic status. Given ethnicity, class and gender, a homogenized notion of 'the Muslim' is undoubtedly *the* most visible of 'others', metaphorically and symbolically.

Virtually all of the young people who enter into the theatre of radicalization and violence do so due to emotional, psychological, ideological and sociological factors. It is thus vital to understand the intersecting paths towards radicalization affecting Islamists *and* far-right extremists to achieve the necessary impact on research, policy and practice. The need to appreciate the dynamics of radicalization as embedded in social processes at the structural level, where concerns over identity, belonging and self-realization, remains fundamental. Invariably, critical thinking and the need to prevent the dehumanization of the 'other' are valuable solutions, particularly in the crucial area of mentoring and support for vulnerable young men within CVE policy. Research on the topic of reciprocal radicalization confirms that processes of 'othering' exist in the minds of angry and disillusioned young men suffering the consequences of the decline of masculinities in an age of globalization. However, instances of mental illness, psychological breakdown and problems concerning self-actualization and self-realization are of importance. Matters relating to terrorism and political violence emanating from far-right and Islamist extremists are regarded as similarly problematic, with both enduring related issues, as the path towards radicalization is often local and urban in nature and outcome. There is a need to recognize that these kinds of extremism are two sides of the same coin, where limiting one will invariably reduce the other. Both extremisms feed off the other's rhetoric, compounding the issue of the diminished status of the privileges of whiteness for many who are facing downward pressures on their social mobility.

Social structure and identity politics are important to take into consideration when attempting to understand the nature of radicalization and extremism among those who engage in far-right extremism as well those drawn to Islamist extremism. Further research is required to understand the intersections of these variables in specific situations. It is vital to examine how understanding these concepts can determine how best they can feed into policy development. Moreover, the approach needs to engage with extremism as a societal issue, not simply as a task for particular communities. It places accountability on government *and* communities to take greater responsibility for the problems *and* the solutions to VE. The following chapter explores the potential ways forward in solving these reciprocal radicalization conundrums.

8

Countering reciprocal radicalization

The far right is increasingly basing its message on an anti-Islamic outlook.[1] During the 2018 Bavarian state elections, an election poster of the Alternative für Deutschland (AfD) showed light-skinned teenagers running down a corridor, using 'Islam-free schools' as their slogan. In several of his speeches, Geert Wilders, president of the Dutch Party for Freedom, claims that Dutch neighbourhoods have been 'Islamized', and according to Marie le Pen, president of the French Front National, 'France is no longer free'. Even though these parties might not directly physically harm others, 'their message is intensified and made explicit in smaller, more extremist groups', such as the Patriotic Europeans against the Islamisation of the Occident (Pegida) and the new European Counter-Jihad Movement (ECJM).[2] Numerous indicators show a rise in extreme-right violence in Europe.[3] A growing number of violent incidents and acts of vandalism in apparent reaction to the construction of Muslim places of worship have been reported in different countries. The terrorist attacks by Anders Breivik, the series of attacks by the National Socialist Underground and the murder of Jo Cox MP are all examples of far-right terrorist attacks committed in Western Europe during the late 2010s. However, acts of violence committed by far-right extremists are still often regarded as isolated events, whereas acts committed by Islamist extremists are more likely to be linked to terrorism and explicit interpretations of the religion of Islam as the primary cause.

Much of the far-right discourse is anti-Muslim to the extent that it is a form of counter-jihad. For some, '[f]ar right extremism is a response to jihadi extremism in society.'[4] However, the reality is that shared local area driving forces and impacts are potentially more important to consider. Moreover, there is 'a wide spectrum of interactional effects and pathways between opposing movements'.[5] This suggests that there are equal sets of relations that define how different groups are radicalized by others, known as reciprocal radicalization. However, several factors hinder writing about reciprocal radicalization. First, far-right extremism, until recently, has been an under-researched field when compared to Islamist extremism, which means that there is limited data available on the two phenomena.[6] Second, many violent acts committed by far-right extremists are classified as 'hate crimes'.[7] Third, there are no universally agreed-on definitions of radicalization and extremism, which restricts comparative analysis. Finally, while the concentration here is on far-right and Islamist extremism, arguably multiple radical right groups are active in contemporary Europe.

Radicalization, extremism and the far right

As established previously, radicalization can refer to a pathway as well as an outcome and does not equate with terrorism per se.[8] These pathways are influenced by a complex variety of factors manifested in several combinations, ranging from global politics to personal issues.[9] Similar issues apply to extremism: some link extremism to the use of physical violence, while others argue that protests can be classified as an act of extremism.[10] This discussion intertwines with a more philosophical debate on what violence entails.[11] Nevertheless, radicalization is universally recognized as an individualized and unpredictable process.[12] The consequence of the subjective nature of the definitions of these notions is that they are dependent on how and when someone classifies an act as radical or extremist behaviour. The judgement of an individual, a group or society depends on its dominant culture, which means that these notions are closely linked to cultural beliefs and perspectives. In the context of Western Europe, this has led to double-standards as acts of far-right extremism tend to be regarded as single events, whereas violent acts committed by radical Islamists are more often linked to networked terrorism. This exclusive focus on Islamist radicalization has been criticized by critics of the contemporary radicalization discourse.

Researching far-right extremism is further complicated by the lack of a clear definition of the movement. Moreover, different labels such as far right, extreme right, radical right alt-right and ultranationalist all refer to a similar phenomenon. Because of the lack of a clear definition, several groups, activities and platforms are categorized as far-right extremist, including 'hate groups, neo-Nazi gangs, white-supremacist movements, nationalist political platforms that espouse anti-immigrant agendas and single issue groups that intensify the tensions between ethnic groups'.[13] Both radicalization and extremism are subjective. The definition of violence is no longer limited to direct physical harm, but includes acts that incite violence, thus broadening the extremist spectrum even further.

The nature of reciprocal radicalization

Fear of Islamist extremism is often mentioned as the trigger for the expansion of the far-right spectrum. However, a more complex set of dynamics are at play as the rise of far-right extremism appears to be more than a counter-action to Islamist extremism, as geographical, ideological and social contexts are all influencing factors in interactive escalations.[14] At first sight, far-right and Islamist extremists seem to be two completely different and opposing groups, but researchers have shown that the two groups seem to have more in common.[15] They share the same local driving forces, such as 'the rise of new subcultures, the decline of traditional masculinity, hate or discrimination, territorial and local claims, grievances, the quest for identity and significance and anti-establishment standpoint',[16] which is associated with their negative perceptions of the consequences of globalization, capitalism and pluralism. In the age of globalization, society has become more individualized, and especially in times of insecurity, such as the economic crisis and refugee crisis, where self-selecting group identities provide a sense of belonging that has otherwise become fractured. Moreover, the similarities do not serve as evidence of reciprocal radicalization but contradict the correlation between religious identity and radicalization.[17]

Aside from the drivers, groups share similar strategies in reaching their goals. They challenge government power, use propaganda, create terror and fear, and send a signal of resistance. By doing so, these movements cause and increase polarization within societies and groups. This shared action frame enables groups to replicate and learn from the strategies of the other, subverting and inverting the actions of others.[18] Right-wing groups, for example, have made use of graphics that depict the beheadings by Islamic State or Muslim women being abused by Islamist groups to justify their hostility towards refugees. This is a process of othering, with identification to the group in opposition to others.[19] Therefore, both Islamist and right-wing extremists construct enemies to define the nature of the people their actions seek to protect and prevent. In this way, they can use the existence of the other to legitimize their raison d'être. This othering is subjective and takes place on multiple levels and between different groups, but both extremist groups are not heterogeneous, as othering takes place within their spectrum. Othering exists within societies but as global culture connects people around the world, extremist groups align themselves to international networks. For example, while members of the public are likely to be aware of the threat posed by organizations such as the Islamic State, they are unaware of groups such as the Identitäre Bewegung, in Germany, which has branches in other EU member states, although the scales of these organizations are hugely different.[20] Moreover, online activities by global networks inspire and motivate individuals who then radicalize in groups. These radicalized few are influenced or motivated by broader networks and ideology through online networks but often prepare and commit violence on their own.[21]

Both extremist groups can be linked to criminal networks and (past) criminal behaviour. For example, one study showed that 40 per cent of Dutch Jihadists had a history of violent behaviour. Similarly, the Bavarian franchise of Pegida 'was organized by two neo-Nazis who were sentenced to prison on terrorism charges in 2003'.[22] Research has established links between far-right networks groups and motorcycle gangs, as well as arms and drug trafficking.[23] Establishing themselves in groups but regularly operating as lone actors, they share the same drivers and use similar strategies to reach their goals.[24] This shared action frame enables them to use the actions of others to legitimize their own, including directly copying their strategies.

Western European politics and society

Researchers have distinguished three waves of right-wing extremism in Europe: the 1960s in France, the 1970s in Italy and the 1990s in Germany.[25] Between 1950 and 2004, Italy, France and Germany experienced most injuries and fatalities caused by this form of VE.[26] In the previous decade, most right-wing terrorist attacks were committed in 2015, mainly in France shortly after the multiple jihadi terrorist attacks the country endured. Similarly, not all countries experience the same rates of jihadi terrorist attacks, with France and the UK being the biggest targets in 2017. This suggests a correlation between the two kinds of terrorist attacks, but due to the complex nature of the problem and lack of data, there is no empirical evidence that clarifies why some countries experience more extremist violence than others. In the Netherlands for example, far-right extremism was mostly directed towards guest workers from Italy and Spain during the 1960s.[27] During the 1970s, the focus shifted towards right-wing extremism directed against Turkish-Dutch and Moroccan-Dutch. In the 1980s, asylum seekers were targeted and during the 1990s, violence was directed against mosques and Islamic objects. However, throughout these years, Jewish groups remained targeted.[28]

Since the start of this century, far-right extremism in Western Europe has 'shifted from the concept of race to that of culture'.[29] Groups such as Pro-Cologne in Germany and Generation Identity in France often align themselves with international networks, 'united by their perception of Muslims and Islam as a threat to their identities, resources and survival of the West'.[30] The majority of the far-right voices are in opposition to Islam and multiculturalism. Members of the EDL in the UK, for example, not only protest against Islam but have 'threatened to stage further demonstrations in areas where local authorities had allegedly refused to use the word Christmas'.[31] However, the changing focus on who the enemy appears to be is problematic for some far-right groups, as they were traditionally focused on animosity towards Jews and Israel.[32] The British National Party (BNP), for example, 'had distributed leaflets warning against the threat of militant Islam in the UK, but a latter issue of the magazine called for bombings against Israeli targets'.[33] Moreover, some counter-jihadist groups, such as the EDL, are involved in football hooliganism.[34] This indicates a focus on multiple enemies, but chants such as 'we all hate Muslims' are a unifying factor for groups like the EDL.

From a historical perspective, Muslims and Islam have been a significant 'other' to European identity ever since the fall of the Ottoman Empire. This is exemplified by the propaganda of the far right that refers to 'the crusades and heroic acts of violence by Christian knights'.[35] In response, Islamist propaganda demonstrates a backlash against traditional values by promoting narrow interpretations of Sharia, reflected in the names of some radical Islamist groups, such as Sharia for Holland. However, multiple issues have been 'successfully exploited by the far right over the last decade'.[36] Aside from the fear of Islam and Muslims, they condemn pluralism, globalization and the EU, fear the presence of immigrants for multiple nationalistic and economic reasons, speak out against the surveillance society and share anger towards other political groups and activists. All factors cause instability and contribute to an environment favourable to the spread of far-right ideologies, where Muslims represent 'one of the many perceived threats'.[37] However, the far-right discourse is voiced within a European political discourse, including in the Netherlands, which shares the suspicious tone towards Muslim communities.[38] During elections, topics such as immigration, integration and Islamization are given more attention than economic.[39] In several Western European countries, the established political actors have even 'adopted some of the elements of the far right in response to the growing organizational strength of the movement'.[40]

The power of opinion

The intersection of media and politics is a significant phenomenon in the Western European discourse on extremism. The murder of Lee Rigby in the UK in 2013, for example, was rapidly determined as an Islamist terrorist attack largely due to the nature of how video and images spread virally. A second meeting of the Civil Contingencies Committee (COBRA) was held in the afternoon of the attack when PM David Cameron cut short his visit to Paris, such was the urgency with which the matter was taken. The media and political exposure given to the event influenced public opinion, with growing concerns expressed over the growth of Islamic extremism in the West. However, it is not only extremism that is feared but Muslims in general. In the UK, 'surveys confirm that large portions of the population (31 per cent) would feel bothered a lot by the presence of an Islamic institution in their community'.[41] This public opinion is reflected in growing support for far-right political parties. Mounting rejection of multiculturalism and rising Islamophobic attitudes enable the far right to gain support because their messages appear more mainstream.[42] Parties link Front National in France and the Party for Freedom in the Netherlands frame their supporters as 'the defenders of equality, liberty and tolerance against their main enemy, Islam, described as a religion of fanaticism and intolerance, incompatible with democratic values and Western culture'.[43] These parties unite in the European Parliament despite their anti-European outlook. A shared enemy connects them.

This othering is based on (inter)national security questions, with the dominant 'war on terror' culture perennially identifying Muslims as the other. The UK government's strategy on CT, for example, has overemphasized Muslim issues, which casts them as suspect communities (see Chapter 9).[44] Thus, the anti-Muslim outlook fits a securitization trend in which immigration and Islam are often discussed regarding security questions, combined with the counter-terror state approach that has concentrated its efforts thus far on the perceived and actual threat from Islamist extremism. However, a positive development is observable, as there seems to be an overall increase in the awareness of the danger posed by far-right extremism. The German government, for example, 'has established a specialist centre focused on far-right and far-left extremism',[45] while Italian policies, for example, still largely focus on religiously motivated extremism.[46] Germany experienced a high influx of refugees, which may be one of the factors for its focus. On the other hand, Italy has not yet experienced religiously motivated terrorist attacks. Therefore, it is difficult to explain what causal factors play a role in this process.

In sum, local and international drivers play a role in the process of othering. The 'enemy' changes over time and, presently, an anti-Islamic outlook drives the messages of the far right. This radicalization discourse is further influenced by questions of security. Even though the message of the radical right is wrapped around Islamophobia, the fear of Muslims is just one of many perceived threats. The political and media discourses possess a problematic tone concerning Muslims, but support for far-right political parties is growing. As local contexts matter, there are observable differences between European countries, but these have not yet been fully explained due to the contextual nature of radicalization.

Countering Reciprocal Radicalization

Thus far, approaches to counter far-right extremism have varied among European countries. They are often dependent upon 'the nature of government in power, [levels of] social cohesion, civil unrest and public opinion towards Muslims'.[47] It is only recently that some countries have begun to tackle both far-right and Islamist extremism under the same CT policy. Therefore, the first step towards policies that tackle reciprocal radicalization is recognition of the threat posed by the far right by all stakeholders, such as internet platforms, the media and governments. Taking the threat seriously is necessary as reciprocal radicalization is often driven by perceived injustice. As both sides of extremism feed off each other's hate and disdain, it is not enough to tackle only one side of the coin. In addition governments must not downplay acts of right-wing extremism as isolated incidents, 'but qualify the acts as hate crimes or ideologically driven violence'.[48] Nevertheless finding the best CT strategy aimed at the early detection of radicalization to counter the risks of terrorism remains an ongoing process as both sides of the extremist spectrum are influenced by biographical factors 'such as proneness to violence; facilitating factors such as violent socialisation via the use of the internet; and triggers such as negatively perceived environmental events'.[49]

First, to tackle violent socialization via the internet, it is necessary to focus on dealing with online activities of radical networks. The narratives and perspectives of the groups embolden each other, and the internet allows people to radicalize. The internet is a vital source of information and inspiration for lone actors. Moreover, as online propaganda spreads fear, it can enhance the polarization of societies and therewith increase perceived grievances on both sides. Therefore, governments 'should cooperate with the private sector companies whose platforms are utilised to share ideas, such as Facebook, Google and Twitter to assess and reassess their internal policies for both hate speech and terrorism'.[50] Monitoring online networks is a useful source of information to help with offline interventions. Second, the interpretation of an environment, which plays a role in perceived and actual grievances, can be influenced by the education of young people; for example, by raising awareness of the refugee crisis to build resistance to reliance on conspiracy theories. It may help to prevent dehumanization of the other. This is important as research on deradicalization suggests that 'dissatisfaction with radical ideologies and networks has a more direct effect on decisions to disengage'.[51] Educating young people might even 'be more effective than creating a counternarrative to the extremist narrative'.[52] Third, to 'prevent the formation of polarising environments that promote violent radicalisation, it is critical to tackle the social disconnection many citizens feel'.[53] The political debate should not enhance polarization, but stimulate participation in society and tackle racism in the labour market. Supporting an open dialogue is arguably more effective than the implementation of repressive measures in countering radicalization. In this regard, key actors may not only be of help in the early detection of radicalization but serve as a connection between the group and society by stimulating open-mindedness.

Reciprocal radicalization between far-right and Islamist extremism is taking place in Western European countries today. While radicalization, extremism and terrorism do not have universal definitions, it complicates the research when these terms essentially remain subjective. Consequently, the interpretation of these events is dependent on who judges. In the Western European context, this has led to considerable research on Islamist extremism, but there is a lack of data on far-right extremism, especially as the discourse of the latter is echoed in political and media discourses, which is in line with the negative public perception of Muslims. Both sides of the extremist spectrum seemingly share more similarities than differences. They are guided by the same enabling factors and use similar strategies to reach their goal. This shared action frame enables the groups to use the actions of the other to their advantage by learning from their strategy and using the actions of their adversaries as a legitimization of the actions and goals of their group.

In Western Europe, the message of the radical right has increasingly become wrapped around Islamophobia. On the one hand, societal rejection of multiculturalism and Islamophobic attitudes have enabled the radical right to gain more influence. On the other hand, public opinion is influenced by the rise of the radical right. This enhances the polarization of society, which fuels both groups. This securitization influences CT policies, which further excludes Muslims and serves as fuel for Islamist extremists. Limiting the opportunities to radicalize and countering or preventing the perceived grievances that can lead to a favourable attitude towards extremist violence is fundamental in countering reciprocal radicalization. Instead of implementing repressive measures, a focus on online activities of radical networks, education of young people to encourage critical thinking and an inclusive society seem more effective to counter reciprocal radicalization. The following chapter offers an examination of the UK's flagship CVE policy framework known as 'Prevent'.

9

The UK 'Prevent' agenda

This chapter situates the 'Prevent' policy debate within the framework of the CVE paradigm, which emerged in late 2015. It is argued that in omitting a nuanced approach to the social, cultural, economic and political characteristics of the radicalized, there is a tendency to introduce blanket measures that inadvertently and indirectly lead to harm. 'Prevent', which has been the outward-facing component of the UK government's counter-extremism strategy since 2006, conflates legitimate political resistance among young British Muslims with indications of VE, providing credence to the argument that 'Prevent' is a form of social control, mollifying resistance by re-affirming the status quo on domestic and foreign policy. In this vicious circle, 'Prevent' adds to *structural* and *cultural* Islamophobia, which are amplifiers of both Islamist and far-right radicalization.[1] 'Safeguarding' vulnerable young people is imperative in this social policy, but the language of inclusion is absent.

New challenges, not so new solutions

The events of 9/11 and subsequent instances of terrorism and VE linked to Islamic radicalism across the world, especially during the rise and fall of the Islamic State (2015–17), have created new challenges without obvious answers. Since the 2015 UN General Assembly, numerous governments have introduced the CVE policy paradigm to prevent, disrupt or generate a counter-narrative to avert, intervene or build community resilience against further instances of VE. As the concept's reach has grown, this policy, known as 'Prevent' in the UK, aims to protect against 'would-be terrorists' based on various assumptions about the sociological, psychological or behavioural characteristics of the 'radicalized'.[2]

'Prevent' is not without its critics in academia, the education sector or among civil society groups. The UK government, however, led by the Home Office, remains steadfast in rolling out 'Prevent', including introducing the Prevent Duty in 2015 to cover a whole host of public sector organizations, in particular in education and health.[3] It is now law for these and other public sector bodies to ensure that they tackle the threats of VE, including reporting on visible differences in appearance in young people, as it is regarded as an indication of radicalization. However, policy limits opportunities to build genuine trust and engagement. It gives succour to far-right extremist movements that grow from how the policy prioritizes Muslim groups. It adds to Islamophobia, both a consequence *and* a driver of further hate, intolerance and VE.

In discussing UK CVE in general and 'Prevent' in particular, the sociological, political and cultural limits of the paradigm can be seen through a left-realist perspective. The left-realist theory originated in the 1970s, at a time of rapid economic transformation as a result of de-industrialization, globalization and technological change, with working class and ethnic minority groups facing the brunt of the decline,[4] which affected hegemonic masculinity,[5] through which male violence emerged as an ecological consequence. The aim here is to gauge perspectives on 'Prevent' within the global CVE paradigm, and the repercussions raised for critical criminology research in this area. In deconstructing these responses, new ways of addressing VE must concentrate energies on localized interventions and engagements, depoliticizing the 'Prevent' and CVE concepts in the process. The problems are local, as are the solutions. Hence, programmatic directives should not define the policy approach from above – but rather through the aspirations of communities in specific localities in the struggle against radicalization from below. British Muslim communities, moreover, need to take greater ownership of both the problem of *and* the solutions to VE – not because Muslims and Islam are the cause of the malaise – but, rather, in the absence of UK government efforts to empower communities, these groups have only themselves to rely on. This is an uneasy task in the current climate of the general disconnect between British Muslims and the state.

The extent and limit of 'Prevent'

From early 2015 to late 2017, the Islamic State carried out numerous acts of VE and terrorism across the world and in the West in particular (including 3 in 4 months in the UK in early 2017).[6] The history of 'war on terror' deradicalization is of policymakers concentrating on religion *and* ideology as both the cause of *and* solution to VE. In the case of Muslim groups, the aim is to resolve problematic religiosity by replacing it with a moderate(d) or a liberal(ized) Islam, in the process instrumentalizing proxy actors drawn from Muslim communities. It includes those who have turned away from Islamic extremism or regressive Islamism, now embracing a postmodern renaissance as so-called newly enlightened Muslims. The focus of this CT approach is to dismantle the mechanics involved in plots, but much of the ideological perspectives determined in the solutions to terrorism have fixated on Islam. The reality is to securitize diversity, focusing on deradicalization based on the notion that individuals move from low-level to vociferous radicalization and, eventually, to violence and extremism. Radicalizers, in reality, mobilize young people attracted to unifying concepts, presented as empowering groups through a holistically conceptualized notion of collective identity that transcends local exclusion and national borders. By portraying their aims as addressing the wrongs that emerge out of the post-war periods of migration and settlement of various Muslim minority groups hailing from lands once under colonial rule, radicalizers focus on racism, inequality, social division and the collapse of multiculturalism or respect for differences in society. However, extremism is a symptom, not a cause of instabilities, insecurities and patterns of anomie experienced by various groups. Here, religion is a convenient umbrella – a suitable instrument of mobilization. It is not the first point of departure in determining radicalization or VE, especially in the diasporic context. Given the limited approach taken by the UK government, Muslim-owned and -led deradicalization initiatives that do not use the language CVE but offer routes to self-empowerment arguably provide greater assistance.

Since its inception, 'Prevent' has encountered various levels of criticism from actors arguing that its agenda is counterproductive and divisive.[7] In 2011, the UK government reviewed its CONTEST (CT strategy), first developed openly in 2006 after the events of 7/7, and from which emerged the 'Prevent' agenda (although it emerged behind the scenes in 2003). This reassessment considered countering ideology central to the battle against terrorism. Moreover, the legal remit of 'Prevent' expanded to emphasize its work alongside different agencies, including health, education and social services. A youth element became a feature of the policy content. As a result the UK government widened its CT strategy to target not just terrorism, but also ideology. Consequently, 'Prevent' re-emphasized the dominant notion of individuals necessarily being on a direct path towards VE as the primary problematic even though it identified a significant conflation between social cohesion and CT. It has led to charges of exclusivism, not inclusivism, and the fostering of existing divisions.[8] The review created two implications for policy. First, the importance of building resilience among communities confronted with radical Islamist extremist narratives. Second, the realization of a specific policing, security and intelligence mandate to engage in overt and covert CT measures, to establish counter-narrative schemes as part of the communication and information battle, and to mitigate the nervousness among government and communities generated by its dissemination. The latter included the significance of building community trust in policing authorities tasked with targeting areas of high Muslim residential clustering and other measures associated with risks of radicalization once connected with a 'Prevent' funding model that allocated budgets based on residential concentration levels of British Muslims.

The toxicity of the 'Prevent' brand is palpable. The 'at risk' versus 'risky' dichotomy blurs ambiguous lines given the politicization of radicalization from above, the consequences of placing too great an emphasis on 'Muslimness'[9] and the structural determinants of radicalization from below. In a paradoxical development, the removal of ethnic inequalities from the mainstream discourse of diversity and difference sees ethnic and religious differences given specific weight in the CT domain.[10] Efforts to clarify the separation between social cohesion and CT add to confusion among politicians and civil servants, proceeding to political and policy paralysis. It intensifies the atmosphere of alarmism towards British Muslims, fanning the flames of far-right sentiment based on anti-immigration, anti-religion and anti-multiculturalism conceptualizations – a 'Muslim paranoia narrative'.[11] A hostile media and political discourse fashions these conditions, deepening and widening the realities of Islamophobia in the process. It leads to levels of violence against Muslims that spike after incidents of terrorism across the world.[12] In a charged and toxic atmosphere, relations between the state and British Muslim communities are restricted, ultimately reduced to a top-down system of design and delivery understood as ideological in design and implementation.[13]

Stigma

The other main concern with 'Prevent' is the mentoring system known as Channel. It implements a one-to-one methodology that works with vulnerable young people to educate, motivate and inspire them away from paths towards VE. The UK government argues that this system prevented several young people from joining the Islamic State as foreign fighters. But it is unable to permit access to original case files or even anonymized case material regarding particular individuals or groups. The Channel model is of interest to other CT agencies across the world, including in France and Germany, with Denmark promoting its unique mentoring approach, known as the 'Aarhus model'.[14] However, whether mentoring alone is the dominating enabler or if a particular mechanism associated with deradicalization from Islamist extremism emerges due to Channel or other similar systems remains unclear. Dealing with terrorism and political violence requires posing complex research questions to generate effective policy interventions.

With so many disparaging voices on the UK government's counter-extremism approach, 'Prevent' endures immense discussion in a charged intellectual, policy and community space. Ongoing concerns relate to impact and effectiveness, but disagreements over the efficacy of the 'Prevent' policy agenda remain. The dominant hegemonic discourse in government policy thinking is to centre on specific interventions regarding British Muslims, in the process alienating a body of people not always able to engage in the political process. For groups without the ability to be the interlocutor that the government encourages, it raises the prospect of 'policed multiculturalism'.[15] With a persistent gaze on terrorism and radicalism, British Muslims are disordered and hesitant about government attempts to engage with groups through this lens of CVE. However, with different groups signalling their interests, the 'Prevent' discourse is the centrifugal force underpinning these counter-competing voices.

The negative discourse on religion in society, in particular on Muslim communities in the West, has a profound effect on stigmatizing communities. First, it creates the impression that Muslim communities are homogenous, powerless and unable to organize themselves against VE. It takes away their agency and narrows the lens through which state–community relations take shape. When governments in Western Europe and North America wish to talk only to their Muslim communities about terrorism and radicalization it causes groups encountering various internal ethnic, sectarian and cultural divisions to disentangle. It raises suspicions that governments are only interested in a type of liberal Islam, which is pro-integration; one based on values and nurturing identities, rather than the structural realities affecting all marginalized communities. Second, the narratives of exclusion and victimization are powerful within the context of Muslim communities still in the process of integrating into society. Much evidence supports claims of exclusion and disadvantage, but it is ignored or relegated to the bottom of the pecking order of social policy priorities, even when it is apparent that radicalizers routinely instrumentalize it in their recruitment of would-be jihadis. This discourse on the 'left behind' concerns the aspirations of former white working-class communities suffering downward social mobility.

Many Muslim groups who came to the West, particularly to Western Europe as part of a post-war migration process, now existing as third and fourth generations, experience numerous instances of economic and cultural alienation. Dominant state actors draw attention to cultural questions within communities concerning such issues as the treatment of women, female genital mutilation or 'grooming' of vulnerable young women. It further distances a body of people looking to the state for answers to structural struggles they suffer as communities within neighbourhoods. Analysis of social media from the Islamic State challenges the assumption that religious narratives encourage vulnerable young people to turn to violent Islamist radicalization to generate answers to their worldly exertions. Less than 10 per cent of its output referred to religion alone.[16] Rather, the likes of Islamic State focused on grievances, which are rooted in the experience of Muslims in the West and the East. With relative ease, it permits radicalizers to play on the injustices of racism and exclusion, vilification in the media, political marginalization and cultural isolation. The present approach to 'Prevent'/CVE, especially in the UK and in other parts of Western Europe, runs the risk of reproducing the very outcomes it wishes to counter.

In understanding the drivers of VE among Muslim communities, and of former white working-class communities who turn to far-right extremism, the symbiotic effects of culture and structure, in addition to the psychological dimensions, generate a systematic understanding of relations between the individual, communities and society. Differences of opinion emerge between state actors and communities, resulting in politicization and polarization, not always prevention or protection. Amid discernible identity claims based on a sense of belonging and the need for participation, acute issues face British Muslim groups who look to the state to respond to the problems facing groups; however, the state is not returning the interest. It indicates institutionalized Islamophobia or anti-Muslim sentiment, which has surfaced as problematic outcomes of the disastrous 'war on terror' and the global 'war on terror culture' that has ensued.

From August 2014 to December 2017, when the Islamic State declared itself as the caliphate, over fifty acts of terrorism across the world were carried out, with Western Europe and North America on the receiving end of many of these attacks. No single profile identifies the archetypical terrorist. Rather, perpetrators are from diverse backgrounds, many of whom have numerous social, economic and cultural apprehensions over their existence as Western Muslims. The unmistakable characteristic is that all of the British assailants implicated in acts of VE, radicalization or terrorism are products of British society.[17] Yet, somehow, policymakers struggle to profile the 'potential violent extremist'. As governments endeavour to promote the notion that vulnerable young people are at risk of radicalization, subsequently committing acts of VE, it stigmatizes an entire group, and disregards instances of political resistance, turning it into *pre-violent extremist criminal thought*, which is policed and securitized, which includes the silencing of legitimate dissent or criticism.

With increasing numbers of young Muslims vulnerable to extremism, it is notable that all were born since the onset of the global 'war on terror'. Contemporary radicalizations are the reality of global issues with local reach. Radicalizers know that their recruitment strategies fill a vacuum, as local leaders are unable to address the concerns of the disaffected young, where much of radicalization reflects on youth rebellion. Broad policy measures advance to a concentration on a narrow range, adding to distrust, and disproportionality. It yields negative consequences due to a heavy-handed, universally directed approach that casts the net far too wide.

Fumbling in the dark

Education is an essential vehicle for change, but education is increasingly securitized. In the process, it stigmatizes existing isolated individuals, especially in schools and in higher education.[18] Prisons are another area of critical research, as they are networking and learning opportunities, as well as spaces targeted by the radicalizers. Overcrowding and pre-trial detention spaces are crucial issues. Those coming out of prisons endure implications for education and employment training. Beyond the UK, the remedy is not a counter-insurgency strategy, but the broader stability of the Middle East in general. In these spaces, a consensus is emerging, but gaps remain in understanding the subtleties of CVE strategies and if they have any impact at all. This omission includes intervention and rehabilitation – that is, detection, recruitment, assessment and evaluation, all involving many layers and levers, including schools, counter-narratives and the pre-criminal space. The concentration on the broad rather than the narrow is the main problem, where the broad refers to public-focused elements and the narrow refers to ideology. Ideology is the tipping point. It takes in young people and it is through debunking ideology that they return to normalcy, but it is separate from religiosity.[19]

Counter-terrorism is an overarching framework that seeks to create a set of policies and interventions that deal with terrorism through active counter-narratives, as well as operational matters of security, policing and intelligence. Counter-extremism is the notion of building community resilience and capability to defend and counteract problematic characteristics affecting threats to national security. Young individuals in the process of donning a hijab or showing attitudinal changes towards specific norms and values, once regarded as an acceptable reality of multiculturalism in the recent past, now face extensive objectification. But the lack of public engagement about 'Prevent' by the UK government creates disengagement on the part of the public concerning the state. For Muslim communities who shoulder acute trials regarding their visibility, in particular for women, additional fears arise. In turn, voices who have little or no opposition or engagement from government or mainstream media fill the anti-'Prevent' vacuum.

As with other countries confronting the threats of VE from groups of a radical Islamist or far-right character, the often-complex but perennial question is how to achieve the balance between individual freedoms and national security. An effort is required to decouple the idea that radicalization is always a security risk or that it will necessarily lead to violence or terrorism. The net result is a 'disconnected citizenship', further alienating religious and ethnic minority groups facing the toxic penalties of an enduring gaze upon them.[20] In reality, polarization poses a greater threat than radicalization, pitching indigenous minority and majority groups against each other. It results in ideological, cultural and political conflict rather than VE or terrorism. The family is crucial, although it is necessary to ensure that attention placed on the household does not promote the 'suspect community' paradigm.[21]

In reality, far-right groups are committing more acts of terrorism relative to their violent Islamist counterparts.[22] The impact of the dysfunctionality of the 'Prevent' programme leads to a breakdown in trust, limiting the opportunities for engagement. However, the power of the state to define the problem *and* the solution is a limited means of policy development, becoming an issue of authoritarian control rather than a social policy seeking to alleviate a problem grasped in collective terms. Further questions on 'Prevent' concern social and political contextualization, measurement and evaluation, and the implications of CT policy. One type of VE should not be a political or policy priority over other kinds, given the range, extent and impact of within-group VE. Questions remain as to whether British citizens are safer due to 'Prevent'. If the risk of VE remains, does it mean that the policy has thus far been unable to deliver on its promise at all? It is discomforting that these questions remain unanswered, especially as 'Prevent' is the brand that the UK exports to the CVE world as a flagship model as well as how it affects British Muslim–state relations in such discernible terms.

Unanswered questions

Since 2010, the UK government has stopped all engagement with the Muslim Council of Britain, the largest and most influential British Muslim umbrella group. It suggests British Muslim communities have to organize themselves in response to Islamophobia and radicalization. In this self-organization, British Muslims are required to take the lead in tackling both Islamophobia and radicalization, not because they are specific Muslim problems, but rather the state is incapable or unwilling to address the precise issues. This is especially the case as current undertakings by the UK government to enhance existing CT legislation have led to accusations of a 'pre-crime' agenda.[23] Much involves behind-the-scenes operations, but the tremendous pressure to produce tangible deliverables leads to an extensive politicization of radicalization, fuelling existing misunderstandings, granting a licence to gross generalizations. Effective intervention needs to be sensitive to the background of every individual to understand where best to introduce interventions. It means the depoliticization of 'Prevent', especially when the approach conflates activism with extremism.[24] A left-realist critical criminological perspective suggests room for deradicalization programmes, but it needs to be community-owned and -led, which means that the present top-down system of selection and processing of individuals for referrals needs to be far more democratic, open and transparent.

British Muslims are under pressure because of the limitations to domestic policy, but 'Prevent' has the consequence of widening divisions and creating further mistrust. The foremost impediment with the top-down 'Prevent' policy is that it is devoid of any real input from the Muslim communities affected by it, apart from predetermined interlocutors straddling divergent communities. The other significant issue with 'Prevent' is the assumption that Islamist terrorism is akin to religious interpretation. It is a useful ruse on the part of commentators and policymakers as it takes attention away from the workings of society, including aspects of institutional, structural and cultural racism, which derives from as well as leads to further Islamophobia. Terrorism is ordinarily about the impact of the deed as a message of defiance of the voiceless: those left behind by the democratic process, those most pushed down by the workings of society and those identified as having the least to offer the rest of society.

The decline in public services since austerity set in in 2010 has plagued Britain. It led the UK government to focus on a particular reading of the *problem* and the *solution*, taking matters back to a time when the general perspective on Islam and Muslims, specifically in the aftermath of the events of 9/11 and 7/7, was negatively focused on religion, culture and identity. The emergence of reactionary and dogmatic policies and programmes, demonizing and vilifying a community or communities, shifts the attention away from specific checks on liberal democracies in the current era, projecting these concerns onto some of the most exposed and vulnerable groups in society. A sense of persecution of a global faith community at the hands of supra-national interests in different parts of the world further blights the judgements of young people with chequered personal histories and troubled lives.

If the focus is only on vulnerabilities, it avoids the stigmatization directed at entire communities and faith groups. It allows practitioners and policymakers to appreciate the holistic dynamics foremost in understanding and limiting VE. It sanctions different sections of society to coalesce around themes that embrace the human condition as a collective experience, avoiding the deleterious consequences of an 'us' and 'them' mentality. The final part of this book explores how potential CVE solutions could emerge in theory and practice.

Part Three

Deradicalization

10

Leaving terrorism behind

Is it possible to persuade terrorists to disengage from violence through non-coercive means? Can one prevent individuals from becoming terrorists through one-to-one interventions? How does one ensure that those convicted of terrorism can reintegrate back into society? How does one guarantee that returnees from the Islamic State do not go on to carry attacks in Western Europe? These are some of the difficult questions being asked by policymakers, academics and communities concerned about preventing individuals at risk of radicalization from carrying out attacks, as well as disengaging individuals from VE. Generically referred to as 'deradicalization', these one-to-one interventions are increasingly seen as desirable in the development of solutions to the threat of VE in many countries. With programmes now found in schools, universities, health sector institutions and prisons, deradicalization remains popular as an instrument of CT policy, with little or no sign of interest abating in the future.

In addition to the term 'deradicalization', these interventions are referred to by several other names, including 'disengagement', 'desistance', 'reintegration', 'rehabilitation' or 're-education'. They are often implemented to reduce the risk of involvement and re-engagement with terrorism. Despite each term denoting a distinct difference in approach and objectives, they commonly describe interventions that aim to increase the resilience and reduce the vulnerabilities of radicalized subjects through a diverse range of measures that include concentration on the psychological, material, social and religious aspects, among others. They are premised on the idea that individuals who are at risk of terrorism, as well as those involved in terrorism, can be redeemed and rehabilitated through non-coercive means. However, it is necessary to distinguish between interventions in the pre-criminal space, on the one hand, and those in the post-criminal space, on the other. This pre-criminal space is concerned with individuals in society who have not committed acts of terrorism or have committed a crime but show signs of being at risk of turning to VE. These approaches have an underlying pre-emptive logic that is not preventive, the aim being to redirect individuals away from a trajectory towards VE. However, the post-criminal space is preoccupied primarily with both convicted and 'at-risk' individuals in prisons, with the assumption that inmates are already violent extremists. The pre-emptive realm appropriates a more rehabilitative in logic but possesses other concerns, such as the potential stigmatization of an entire group (see Chapter 9 as a case study of the UK 'Prevent' agenda).

The majority of these pre-crime interventions in the pre-criminal space are based on voluntary involvement of individuals; however, there has emerged a new requirement of 'mandatory' deradicalization for specific cases resulting from the return of women, children and foreign fighters from Islamic State back to their countries of birth. The proliferation of these interventions in CVE and CT regimes is due to their attractiveness as policy options. For policymakers, it is seen as good risk management: in the pre-criminal space, it assists in preventing the recruitment and radicalization of a new generation of terrorists by turning off the tap of potential recruits. In prisons, the aim is to reduce the risk of re-engagement of militants who have been reintegrated back into mainstream society. It addresses the problem of prison radicalization, which is a prominent recruitment hotspot for would-be terrorists. This pre-crime approach is proactive and precautious, intending to reduce the risk of terrorism in the future. Its appeal is particularly salient considering the challenges of dealing with the returnees from Islamic State to their home countries. What does one do, for example, with the return of children, women and foreign fighters? What is it to be done in the absence of evidence to prosecute? Given that many returnees will not pose a security risk, while conversely, the minority of returnees that do present a risk represent a serious threat, how are they to be reintegrated back into their communities? Policymakers have turned their attention to the pre-crime opening as a solution to these challenges.

There are vast differences regarding how these programmes should be administered, who implements them, what should be their aims and what works. Many governments and civil society practitioners agree about the goal – which is to reduce the risk of terrorism – but disagree about how to get there. The various target groups, the multiple stakeholders, the different types of interventions, problems of concepts and definitions and the fact that these interventions touch upon sensitive issues relating to security adversely impact the vital prerequisite qualities of trust, transparency and access needed by them to develop and improve all culminate in a complex policy field. A major underlying reason for the complexity characterizing these issues is related to the amorphous and rapidly changing security threat in many countries, as well as the maturation and evaluation of a policy field that started to take shape in the late 1990s and early 2000s. Because of this complexity, understanding it academically, implementing it in practice and evaluating its effects have become very challenging.

This chapter has two aims. First, to elucidate the evolution of these interventions by examining the underlying concepts supporting them and the development of the approaches and methods currently employed in the field. Second, to analyse four central challenges facing them: (1) the disjuncture between what is known about why people leave terrorism behind and the difficulties of implementing this knowledge at a programmatic level; (2) the challenges involved in measuring interventions and proving that they work; (3) the deficiencies inherent in dominant conceptions governing the implementation of interventions; and (4) the disjuncture between what is known historically about how armed groups transition away from terrorism and the current efforts concerning deradicalization. It is clear, however, that these interventions are fraught with conceptual and practical intricacies. In addition, in terms of monitoring and evaluation, they are divorced from the social process that sustains VE and the absence of understanding the impact of a sense of injustice and misplaced politics that drives VE.

To deradicalize or disengage

Deradicalization is the social and psychological process where the commitment of an individual to and his or her involvement in VE is reduced to the extent that they are no longer at risk of involvement in violent activity.[1] Essential to understanding the concept of deradicalization in practice is the notion of a cognitive shift, that is, a fundamental change in understanding on the part of those affected by radicalization. At the heart of the deradicalization hypothesis is the principle that ideas have causal agency and that behavioural change in individuals occurs through ideas. However, deradicalization poses several challenges for practitioners. First, the term 'deradicalization' is often conflated with other similar ideas and interventions. The term 'deradicalization' is erroneously used as a broad, catch-all term to encompass other different but related methods and techniques aimed at reducing the risk for society due to terrorism, such as 'countering violent extremism' (synonymous with 'counter-radicalization') and 'preventing violent extremism' (synonymous with 'anti-radicalization'). Second, the objective of deradicalization is complex because it implies that interventions can only be successful if radicalized individuals change their views and beliefs, which has proved to be a demanding objective to accomplish. Third, determining the change in views and beliefs of individuals is problematical because they cannot be measured and tested. Finally, research indicates that ideational and ideological factors play little or no role in persuading individuals to enter or leave such groups and movements.[2]

In contrast to deradicalization, disengagement aims at changing the behaviour of offenders, namely the cessation of terrorism. It is defined as, 'the process whereby an individual experiences a change in role or function that is usually associated with a reduction of violent participation'.[3] Disengagement is premised on the notion that behavioural change precedes transformations in ideas and beliefs and that changing the ideas and beliefs of offenders is ineffective on its own in stopping individual engagement in terrorism. Rather, disengagement should be accompanied by other provisions (e.g. social support, material incentives and other inducements). Disengagement is unworkable as an interventional goal. On balance, it is problematic to accurately measure and test changes in belief scientifically, whereas changes in behaviour, a changing role for individuals within a terrorist group, with an individual disconnecting from other terrorists or simply walking away from terrorism, are easier to assess as intervention objectives. Currently, pre-crime interventions are aimed primarily at behavioural change over and before the cognitive change. In the mid- to late 2000s, these interventions were associated with the term 'deradicalization' and cognitive change was the objective. Since then, the field has adopted the objective of behavioural change over cognitive change, of disengagement before deradicalization. This is due not only to the problems characterizing deradicalization, as outlined above but because of the merits of disengagement as a more workable approach. It eschews the terminological and conceptual challenges of deradicalization and stresses the concentration on individual engagement and support for terrorism instead of the slippery terrain of ideas and beliefs. Moreover, changes in behaviour are more amenable as an intervention objective. There are thus worthy reasons for this shift from deradicalization as an organizing concept to an intervention objective towards disengagement.

Meanwhile, terms such as 'desistance' and 'reintegration' have gained traction in recent years. While these terms are interchangeable with 'deradicalization' and in particular 'disengagement', both 'desistance' and 'reintegration' mark not only distinct logics but also an evolution of the thinking surrounding deradicalization and disengagement. Adopted from the more established field of crime prevention and in the United States, 'desistance' denotes the process by which individuals cease criminal activity or offending.[4] Reintegration meanwhile is understood as a safe transition into the community, by which the individual proceeds to live a law-abiding life following his or her release, and acquires attitudes and behaviours that generally lead to productive functioning in society.[5] While disengagement and deradicalization emphasize the cessation of violence, the subtle yet critical point is that 'disengagement is actually about engagement somewhere else'.[6] For disengagement to work, it means individuals have to engage with a new life elsewhere. In other words, while lip service is paid to the notion of reintegration, the core objective of pre-crime interventions was, until recently, on getting individuals to *move away from violence* (disengagement and deradicalization), which precluded the additional paramountcy of moving positively towards a new life (reintegration). Disengagement and desistance represent one side of the equation and reintegration the other side.

In many ways, reintegration or 'pro-integration' is a two-way process in which both society and the individual play a role in producing successful outcomes.[7] Here, reintegration is understood as re-entering a specific community setting, with people who know the individual. This is more nuanced than the reintegration of ex-offenders into the ambiguous and amorphous notion of 'community' or even the more hazy term, 'mainstream society'. Such distinctions are not merely semantic but result in a real difference in how policies are implemented. Reintegration, thus, has a more positive connotation than deradicalization given that it means that these interventions converge on helping offenders find and settle into an alternative pathway in life. Reintegrating terrorist offenders thus requires a holistic and long-term approach reliant on society's role in helping them return to normal life and not just about persuading individuals to leave terrorism behind. Another development in recent thinking on desistance and reintegration is the move towards 'strength-based' approaches in the UK with its Desistance and Disengagement Programme (DDP), as well as variants to the Aarhus model in Denmark, where the emphasis is on empowering individuals with the social skills for reintegration. The difference between the majority of deradicalization and disengagement programmes on the one hand and 'strength-based' approaches, on the other hand, is that the former centre on risk reduction whereas the latter is person-centric.[8] Risk-based interventions have been criticized for neglecting the contextualized social embeddedness of people's lives, concentrating instead on risk factors and profiles in assessments of offenders. This attention to risk has affected the attraction of intervention in relation to prisoners because it neglects personal motivation.[9]

The 'strength-based' approach is predicated on the assumptions that individuals are motivated to pursue several goods, for example, achievement and positive relationships. According to this theory, ideology is the interpretive framework that individual agents employ to decide what to pursue and how to pursue it. Within this framework, terrorism involves pursuing 'goods' that break social and legal norms, whereas disengagement is over the 'growing commitment to achieving goods in ways that society deems acceptable'.[10] The focus on 'strength-based' approaches is on re-directing the goals of extremists in pro-social rather than illegal ways. For example, if the individual were motivated by helping their co-religionists, this would thus entail finding how the individual can achieve this outcome through alternative means. Consequently, this approach does not require de-constructing their ideological motivations for involvement or engagement with terrorism. The goal of reintegration is on facilitating sustainable ways in which individual agents can pursue their goals.

Intervention tools and approaches

The interventions discussed above employ a range of activities, approaches and tools to change behaviour. A combination of methods must be deployed to ensure that individuals disengage from terrorism. There are roughly seven tools, outlined below:

1. **Ideational:** this approach targets the ideas and values of participants. It involves theological refutation of ideas and

legitimization of other ideas within a religious framework. Activities include counter-theology, counter-ideology and debate. It often involves violent extremist leaders, mentors, imams, caseworkers and religious leaders.

2. **Material:** this relates to providing material support to detainees, in terms of finding them a home or employment, as well as severing the material reliance of individuals on VE networks.
3. **Pastoral:** in the pre-crime space, this takes the form of mentoring. In the prison context, detainees receive pastoral care through caseworkers and imams.
4. **Vocational:** vocational rehabilitation is concerned with preparing offenders to reintegrate into society with skills development and educational attainment.
5. **Psychology**: psychological rehabilitation involves psycho-profiling and assessment of individuals and providing participants or detainees with support, for example, counselling and therapy.
6. **Social:** social approaches are about aiding the family of the captured terrorist as well as getting family and friends increasingly involved in the disengagement process.
7. **Sanctioning:** the use of sanctions, specific to the post-crime space, refers to how, for some governments, the reintegration of offenders back into society is contingent on mandatory participation in various interventions. In some non-democratic regimes, this takes the form of threats, such as the removal of privileges or the threat of punitive responses.

Often, these interventions employ more than one type of activity, tool and approach, with different causal mechanisms operating in different contexts. This multi-pronged approach is premised on the notion that there is no silver bullet or single approach that works. This partly stems from the fact that because these interventions include both material and counter-ideological component it is perplexing to evaluate which factors are the most vital.[11] Furthermore, the use of multiple approaches acknowledges the highly individualized reality of disengagement from violence, as every individual is different. It is interconnected to the growing prevalence in the field that interventions must be tailor-made to suit the individual.[12] However, the application of tailor-made approaches is affected by the locale in which the intervention takes place, the resources available for the intervention, as well as the sex and age of participants/detainees.[13] To elaborate further, the decline of the Islamic State in 2018 meant that many countries have had to deal with the unforeseen security, political and social challenges of the return of women ('Jihadi Brides') and/or children ('Cubs of the Caliphate'). These interventions have been seen increasingly as the solution to this problem and yet they have not developed until now to address the challenges presented by women and children returning from Islamic State and the potential threats they pose (or otherwise). Moreover, this challenge for administering interventions is complicated by other factors: namely the fact that resources and expertise vary not only between countries but also between municipalities within countries. Thus, while tailor-made approaches are crucial for the success of interventions, they nevertheless present methodological challenges in implementation.

Tailor-made approaches entail administering different types of interventions for each case. The notion here is that the interventions address the specific personal circumstances and motivational factors of the individual concerned. Consequently, individuals are assessed to identify their motivations for engaging with terrorism. Mainstream psychology has shown that it is possible to hold extreme beliefs and be non-violent, while some violent extremists have not been influenced strongly by ideology.[14] For some individuals, therefore, their involvement may be ideological but for others, their motivations could be social, such as the need to belong to a group. Furthermore, a minority may have mental health issues, while others may not have the skills to reintegrate back into society. There are also differences in how interventions are applied between leaders and followers. Understanding the highly individualized approach to disengagement does away with ineffectual cookie-cutter generic approaches. Increasingly, in the pre-criminal space in Western European countries, these interventions are implemented through multi-agency partnerships. The UK, Denmark and the Netherlands have developed their CVE programmes upon their existing crime prevention infrastructure, where the police have had experience working through multi-agency approaches to prevent crime. This is based on the collaboration of the probation services, school, colleges, universities, hospitals and other representatives of state institutions in panels to address youth crime. This multi-agency approach is developing in America, Canada and Australia. They have the advantages of decentralizing interventions, encouraging the participation of civil society and a whole society approach to CVE.

In the global south, the development of multi-agency approaches to CVE faces challenges. They require the existence of strong institutions and the availability of the right expertise and resources, which are prerequisites missing in developing countries. There are other essential capacity-building elements required, for example the training of prison officers, mentors and other experts, the development of risk assessment procedures and documentation, and the consideration of monitoring and evaluation of interventions, all of which require money, time, procedures and expertise often in short supply. An additional challenge pertains to the role of civil society in CVE. In many countries, civil society is crowded out by the state and the state does not trust civil society to deliver. In countries like Pakistan, which has various deradicalization programmes, the military and not the police are used in administering such programmes.[15]

Other critical contextual factors are influencing the unique development of interventions in countries often mediated by what is permitted culturally and politically. The programme in Saudi Arabia, for example, has provided inmates with wives as part of their deradicalization efforts, a measure possible only in a tribal and conservative society. The top-down state interventions in the sphere of religion in places such as Morocco, Egypt, Saudi Arabia and Jordan would not be possible in secular liberal European societies. The Hayat model in Germany is inspired by their experience fighting far-right VE and the discovery there that the role of family and friends in helping radicals disengage is embraced by current interventions targeting Islamist-inspired terrorism.[16] The much-acclaimed Aarhus model in Denmark emphasizes the importance of social integration, as well the skills needed by individuals to secure key social goods in their lives. This approach grows out of the Danish egalitarian ethos. Culture is hence significant in shaping the development of programmes and setting the parameters of what can be tried and implemented.

Implementing interventions

A lot more is known about why individuals join VE groups than why they leave them; however, knowledge about why individuals leave terrorism behind is not well developed or conceptualized. Over the past decade, the CVE space has attempted to learn from the experience of other fields: desistance from crime, disaffiliation from cult groups, exit from right-wing groups and disengagement from terrorism.[17] The evidence base shows that there are diverse and highly individualized reasons explaining why individuals leave terrorism, much of which has very little do with intellectual content such as ideology and beliefs or even material incentives and more to with psychological and social issues. However, there remains a disconnect between what we know in the nascent yet growing *scholarship* on the subject on the one hand and what is being implemented in *practice* on the other hand. Based on interviews with terrorists, two factors of disengagement are identified: psychological and physical. The psychological include disillusionment arising from incongruence between the initial ideals and fantasies that shape a person's initial involvement and their subsequent experiences with the reality of what is entailed by involvement; disillusionment arising from disengagement over tactical issues; disillusionment arising from strategic, political or ideological differences; burn out; and changing personal priorities.[18] Physical factors include a voluntary exit from the movement; involuntary exit from the movement; an involuntary movement into another role; a voluntary movement into another role; involuntary exit from the movement altogether; and experiences stemming from psychological disengagement that acts as a catalyst for physical disengagement.[19] Arrest, imprisonment and death are identified as the most dramatic examples of physical disengagement. These psychological and physical factors can therefore either become linked, occur independently or converge. Moreover, a salient point about this process is that the occurrence of these factors does not necessarily lead to complete and total disengagement; it may lead instead to 'role change'.[20] In this instance, the individual may renounce violence but remain active in the activities of the group in another way or role. For example, a known IRA militant moved away from a militant role to a political role in Sinn Féin.[21]

In terms of disengagement from extremists–right-wing groups, a distinction between *push* and *pull* factors can be made.[22] *Push* factors include:

- Negative social sanctions that may cause some to reconsider their affiliation. These may range from parental scolding and social isolation to criminal persecution and harassment;
- Some lose faith in the ideology and politics of the group or movement;
- A feeling that 'things are going too far';
- Disillusionment with the inner workings and activities of the group;
- Losing confidence, status and position in the group; and
- A feeling of exhaustion and that they can no longer take the pressure.

Pull factors, in contrast, refer to aspects attracting the person to a more rewarding alternative. They include:

- A longing for the freedoms of normal life;
- Activists feeling they are getting too old for what they are doing;

- Activists caring about career prospects and personal futures; and
- Establishing a family with new responsibility for a spouse and children.

Concerning desistance from crime, most studies highlight the following correlative dynamics of desistance: positive relationship/family;[23] change in personal identity; maturation (outgrowing the group and the cause); and stable legal employment. Meanwhile, desistance from terrorism (a much newer question in the field) suggests that de-legitimizing ideology, failing credibility of an organization, disillusionment with leadership or group structure, and a change in practical life circumstance are important considerations. As the evidence base illustrates, abandoning terrorism at the individual level has little to do with religion, ideology and material incentives. The literature shows that 'push-factors' better indicate the likelihood of disengagement than 'pull-factors',[24] with the feeling of disillusionment over strategy, tactics or leadership highlighted as the most commonly attributed reason to initiate exit from.

The prominence of 'push' factors suggests that the priority of interventions should be on addressing psychological and social considerations, particularly in promoting disengagement frames that facilitate the sense of disillusionment with the group. For example, the message of the disengagement frames should highlight how divided the organization and movement is; emphasize the disjuncture between the facts on the ground and the ideology of the group; stress the failure, abuse or corruption of the leadership of the group; discourage acts of terror due to its tactical and strategic futility; and stress the group's directionlessness.[25] While these frames may touch upon religious and ideological content, they nevertheless play a secondary role in the psychological and social components that motivate and drive the disengagement process. However, in practice, interventions are constrained by multiple reasons (political agendas, resources, assumptions and so on) that impede the adoption of state-of-the-art knowledge in this space. Furthermore, many interventions remain preoccupied with counter-ideology and theological refutations. Much of what motivates individuals to leave terrorism seems to be highly individualized or due to issues outside the ability of interventionists to control and effect, for example the level of investment the individual has placed in the group and the cause. The reality is that even if one knows everything about leaving terrorism behind, that is the when, how and why, this would not translate practically into programming. How the intervention processes work in practice is more complex than the 'push'/'pull' framework suggests. Besides the elements that lead individuals to leave terrorism behind, there are several important dimensions to consider when understanding the process, all of which make administering interventions successfully taxing, which explains why abandoning terrorism remains challenging.

An individual's satisfaction levels ('push' factors) or the appeal of an alternative life ('pull' factors) do not solely determine an individual's commitment to the group and the cause, but the level of investment, which is the most imperative variable that determines the commitment level to a relationship. This is not necessarily the level of satisfaction or the availability of potential alternatives. In the context of a commitment to terrorism, this is because both intrinsic and extrinsic investments are potentially lost if the individual leaves the group and movement. The bigger the investment, the more likely people are to stay in relationships. Terrorism, after all, is a high-risk activity in which individuals are tied not only through romantic and familial bonds but through intense shared experiences, memories and emotions. Given that individuals in terrorist organizations have shunned the outside world and have invested fully in in-group relationships, the investment model predicts that leaving terrorism is extremely costly to individuals, even when they are dissatisfied, and even when alternative lifestyles look appealing. The following chapter explore further these strategies in order to understand their effectiveness in reality.

11

Disordered deradicalization

Deradicalization interventions must contend with highly individualized processes, which are characterized in real life by transitions, lapses and relapses. This dynamic may include a shift in the role and the identity of the group than a finite step. Therefore, rather than view leaving terrorism as a finite step, deradicalization interventions should be viewed in the field as a dynamic process resulting in several outcomes. This is reflected in the criminal desistance literature[1] and disaffiliation from new religious movements.[2] Many disengaged individuals may return to terrorism, although very little is known about recidivism in the terrorism literature.

Deradicalization is not a linear process of stages but a meandering journey, with no final or fixed outcome. It occurs over a long period – in some cases, many years. Disengagement from terrorism is not necessarily a permanent state. It is more accurate to view it in terms of a conditional arrangement, one dependent on political events. For example, in a study based on a series of interviews with current and former members of Islamist jihadist group in Indonesia, many stated a willingness to fight if sectarian conflict re-emerged in Central Sulawesi or Maluku province.[3] This is an example of a 'conditional disengagement frame' in which violence is only delegitimized in certain places and time while being legitimized in other contexts;[4] for example, offensive jihad is delegitimized but defensive jihad against an occupying force is legitimate. Individuals may choose to abandon terrorism at one time and re-engage at another, depending on the social and political context.

Equally significant is the fact that former militants can remain committed to the ideas and ideology of their militant past and yet be fully reintegrated into society. This was shown in a study of nine former militants from the Ulster Volunteer Force and two from the Red Hand Commando in Northern Ireland. It suggests that the deradicalization component of disengagement, that is, ideological revision, is, in fact, less important than delegitimizing violence. Two versions of deradicalization, one broad and the other narrow, are defined here. For example, during the height of Islamic State, the removal of Western influence from the Middle East and the validity of armed struggle made it likely for them to engage in or support an armed struggle. But with the narrow perspective, an actor's belief in the validity of armed struggle alone makes it likely for them to engage in or support armed violence.[5] The narrow perspective of deradicalization suggests that disengagement can be achieved by delegitimizing violence, which is sufficient to reduce the risk of re-engagement with terrorism. In terms of deradicalization interventions, this means it may be more constructive to focus on delegitimizing the violence rather than deconstructing the ideological framework that underpins it.

Often underplayed in discussions of deradicalization is the paramountcy of cultivating a new identity. To leave terrorism behind, ex-offenders must start a new life, carve out a new identity and reintegrate back into familial and social structures. This is an exceptionally challenging phase in the journey to becoming an 'ex'-terrorist. The barriers individuals face when trying to begin a new life are both internal to the individual and existential, but also external (i.e. an individual's relationship to the social world). Both are questions that deradicalization interventions are not equipped to address given the complexity, resource-draining and time-consuming nature of forming a new identity. These challenges are compounded in some situations by the unwillingness of communities to accept the reintegration of former combatants, as evidenced in Nigeria's deradicalization programme, where former combatants have been killed or pushed away.

Both the ex-terrorist and individual at-risk of radicalization need to settle the question of purpose and identity. Disengagement is about engagement somewhere else, for individuals cultivating a new or secure identity are required to acquire meaningful commitments. Such obligations should act as a substitute for the intense commitments their previous lives offered, which were characterized by intense bonds of belonging, sacrifice and purpose – matters difficult to replicate when returning to normal life. Commitment, therefore, requires a shared understanding of what is worth pursuing. In the case of ex-offenders, they need to rebuild a new social life: they must find employment, develop a new social network and complete mundane tasks, which they will struggle with, such as opening a bank account. They may have to rebuild burnt bridges with significant others, start new relationships and acquire new skill sets for employment, social interaction and even to be able to regulate their own lives. The cultivation of a new identity, therefore, requires not only abandoning an older identity but also adopting new commitments.

Monitoring and evaluation

A major challenge facing deradicalization intervention is evaluating whether particular interventions work. How does one measure behavioural change? How can one know that individuals have deradicalized? The first challenge is identifying the goals of interventions, which may well be diverse in reality. The objective is either to prevent radicalization (with individuals not yet radicalized) or to mitigate radicalization (with individuals already radicalized); whereas the goal of deradicalization in the criminal space is to disengage radicalized individuals from a violent extremist group or to suppress radical behaviour of individuals through detention and prohibition. These interventions distinguish between different phases of radicalization – preventive, suppressive or restorative – and can be broken down into short-, medium- and long-term periods. This diversity of goals and time make it challenging to assess the effects of interventions. For example, some interventions may have more than one purpose, particularly because the line between prevention and mitigation can be blurred. In addition, the periods affect the goals of interventions. It is not clear how short-time frames (under a month) work and whether they have any effect. Some deradicalization programmes in prison, like the Saudi programme, are based on long-term (more than a month) restorative interventions. Much fewer interventions aim at suppressing radicalization. Most interventions found in counter-radicalization programmes operate in the pre-crime space, like 'Prevent' and the Danish programmes, and have long-term goals. The problem, however, with long-term goals is that the methods for monitoring and evaluating interventions are not directed towards measuring long-time spans.

Given the diversity of focus and vague multi-layered policy objectives, it is tricky to formulate indicators of success that relate concrete measures that impact on recipients.[6] Many expected outcomes of interventions involve ephemeral changes related to cognition and opinion, which are taxing to rigorously track, especially when there is a paucity of secure baselines for comparison. But even if one could track changes in views through perception surveys taken before and after the intervention, it would not be sufficient in itself to gauge actual cognitive change. Participants involved in the intervention may superficially communicate to caseworkers and intervention providers what may appear to be the right responses to such assessment to show progress and comply with the programme. Furthermore, while behavioural change is a better indicator of success and arguably a clearer manifestation of cognitive change, it is hard to ascertain. Behavioural change often takes years to occur, which is beyond the capacity of most interventions to measure; meanwhile, by a similar token, the behavioural change that occurs quickly, suddenly or within a short period has its drawbacks. For example, the change may be cosmetic and not substantial or even due to expedience rather than principle; or it may be genuine but not been instantiated in the life habits and circumstances of the individual long enough and who, therefore, risks relapsing.

It is challenging to evaluate deradicalization interventions because most programmes do not clearly outline the mechanisms or assumptions about how the intervention will bring about the desired change (referred to as the theory of change). Theories of change are an explanation of how the desired change will take place, linking the goal of interventions with their outcomes, activities and inputs. These theories explicitly identify linkages, improve planning, and allow evaluators to measure the progress and impact of the intervention. To understand the intervention logic, it is important to comprehend the behaviour associated with VE and the relevant levers for change. For the former, it is essential to understand the theoretical approach and assumptions used to explain VE (e.g. social identity theory, social movement theory and conveyor-belt theory). The key here is identifying the assumptions that intervention providers have regarding radicalization and how to affect it. This includes understanding the factors of VE, the type of change in behaviour desired (whether behavioural or attitudinal or both) and the existing challenges or limitations in place to achieving the necessary behavioural change.

With regard to the levers for change, interventions need to identify the various tools that encourage behavioural change, for example, through legislation that restrict an individual's movement, or through incentives such as assisting individuals to improve their skills or find a job, as well as through supportive interventions like counselling. Understanding levers of change requires comprehending the various beneficiary targets of the intervention (individuals, groups, community, civil society, prison inmates or frontline staff) as well as an appreciation of the unintended effects of the levers of change. Another critical challenge in monitoring and evaluating deradicalization interventions is attribution. To what extent is the change in outcome attributable to the intervention? This is the problem of attribution, as it attempts to isolate the link between causal factors and intervention outcomes. However, the lack of short (and manageable) causal chains renders it difficult to exclude rival explanations. The programmatic logic of an intervention or its 'theory of change' can often become incoherent as the path from delivery to impact on target groups is 'long and winding'.[7] This is complicated by the fact that observed changes could partly be the result of the intervention in the best-case example. In reality, the context, the environment and a litany of other variables will affect the intervention. Isolating the intervention or variable that leads to the behavioural change is hugely problematic.

Causality is further complicated by the reality that intended outcomes in the pre-crime space usually involve 'nothing happening'. This is linked to another challenge: the counter-factual. After all, in the pre-crime space, individuals are not terrorists. They are simply 'at risk'. Analysing attribution requires comparing the situation 'with' an intervention to what would have happened in the absence of an intervention. This is challenging because it is not possible to observe how the situation would have been without the intervention. Another issue is that in the pre-crime space, given that engagement is voluntary and based on consent, individuals taking part are already willing to change. The sample of individuals undergoing interventions is thus self-selecting. It is difficult to evaluate the intervention using treatment and control groups because of messy conditions, ethical constraints and a lack of resources. It makes it difficult to identify the causal variable of change scientifically.

Finally, there is a major lack of empirical evaluation of interventions. Governments have been reluctant to release information on these programmes,[8] which makes it difficult to know whether interventions have worked and why. Data is often anecdotal and descriptive, making inferences about the potential impact conjectural, dependent on narrative interpretations and difficult to validate. Many evaluations concentrate on programmatic outputs instead of the outcome. But the output is a quantifiable measure of what the intervention has produced and, therefore, offers no substantive assessment on the effectiveness of projects beyond superficial benchmarks that do not account for externalities or long-term impact. Moreover, most interventions are evaluated internally by providers or a delivery agency and not by an independent external party. Even academic attempts at evaluating prison deradicalization programmes rely heavily on the descriptions, information and account provided to them by the government or agency delivering the intervention. Information sharing relies on a culture of transparency and receptivity, which is challenging when the data is sensitive and heavily regulated.[9]

How terrorism ends

A major challenge for deradicalization interventions is the fact that they do not fit into a theory and evidence base for how terrorist campaigns come to an end and how groups transition from armed struggle to non-violence. Predominantly, the focus of most interventions is on the individual and not organizations and social movements. Yet terrorism is a social phenomenon sustained by groups, organizations and social movements. There are historical examples demonstrating that terrorism comes to end by focusing efforts on preventing individuals from becoming terrorists; and while there are influential militant leaders renouncing violence in, for example, Egypt, Algeria and Northern Ireland, these cases of disengagement have taken place within the context of collective disengagement, a political opportunity for disengagement and the idiosyncratic dynamics unique to the context in which disengagement takes place. History shows that terrorist campaigns come to an end even though terrorism does not. It is undeniable that the turn towards deradicalization and disengagement of individuals in the late 2000s was a useful and beneficial corrective and vital addition to the body of knowledge. However, it is illuminating nevertheless that the contemporary focus on individual deradicalization does not have precedence in the literature. Research highlights the interplay between internal (organizational dynamics) and external factors (political context) in the evolution of terrorism.[10] Ostensibly, the end of terrorism may result from one or more of the following situations:

- **Success:** accomplishing objectives;
- **Preliminary success:** achieving public recognition for an organization and the causes it espouses;
- **Organizational breakdown:** if recruitment and resources dry up, the organization may not be able to sustain itself;
- **Dwindling support:** organizations may lose the support of their various constituencies, the populations they seek to represent and the governments or other organizations that support them;
- **New alternatives:** at times, other options for political change emerge. They can include more traditional warfare or revolution, mass protests or political negotiations.

In other research, there are at least seven broad explanations for or critical elements in the decline and end of terrorist groups in the modern era.[11] They are:

1. Capture or killing of the leader;
2. Failure to transition to the next generation;
3. Achievement of the group's aims;
4. Transition to a legitimate political process;
5. Undermining of popular support;
6. Repression; and
7. The transition from terrorism to other forms of violence.

All of these perspectives underscore the degree to which terrorist groups evolve independently of government action, but the result is a strong bias towards tying the decline of such groups to specific government policies.[12] Other theories examining the decline of terrorism emphasize the role of the life cycle of movements and organizations. The influential theory of terrorism waves posits that modern terrorism has undergone four waves, each characterized by a distinctive use of tactics and weapons, which declines and then gradually gives birth to a new wave. The four waves are the Anarchist wave (1878–1919), the Anti-Colonial wave (the 1920s–early 1960s), the

New Left wave (mid-1960s–1990s) and the Religious wave (1979–the present).[13] But history shows that terrorist campaigns end even though terrorism does not. Others have explored the applicability of a conflict theory framework to the longevity of terrorist groups, including stages of emergence, escalation and de-escalation. In similar vein to the notion that terrorism comes in waves, terrorism is seen as contingent on the life cycle of the terrorist group.[14]

However, an objection to the argument that terrorist organizations and campaigns come to an end due to internal factors or that the role of government policy has been exaggerated in that deradicalization interventions do not aim to bring terrorism to an end but are about managing risk. Risk management is an acknowledgement that one cannot eliminate terrorism but can only contain it and reduce it to an acceptable level. Naturally, some will inevitably escape surveillance. Risk itself can never be eliminated, only reduced. Even in Northern Ireland, the most intensively monitored territory in the Western world in the 1980s and 1990s, bombs still went off.

Disengagement as a social process

The essential problem with deradicalization interventions in reducing the risk of terrorism is that they only address symptoms and not the sociological context that facilitates political violence. They target individuals and not groups and networks. Yet terrorism is a social phenomenon, dependent on a community and movement. It is not the result of individual decisions to adopt an extremist ideology. Even if a few individuals are disengaged from political violence and are successfully reintegrated into society, it will not necessarily reduce the risk of political violence against the state if there remains a politicized organization and movement committed to the struggle. The movement writ large will continue to inspire and attract recruits to its cause. This would suggest, then, that the focus of preventive interventions should be on networks, groups and the movement if attempts by governments to stymie the next generation of terrorists are going to be successful. Or, at least it suggests that focusing solely on the transformation of individuals through technical interventions will not work on its own.

The significant role of organizational and social movement transformation required in the disengagement process is highlighted in several studies.[15] Indeed, disengagement was conceptualized as a social process in the earliest study of deradicalization.[16] The study found similarities in the evolution of German social democracy and Soviet communism, with deradicalization signifying a subtle change in their relations to the social milieu.[17] Deradicalization occurs when a movement 'comes to terms with the existing order' and accepts the established system and institutional procedure.[18] Crucially, it was found that the involvement of communist parties in democratic electoral politics made them more pragmatic, non-heretical and non-ideological.[19] A similar conclusion was reached in a more recent study analysing radical social movements in the Netherlands.[20] The study concluded from their examination of the radical Moluccans, the Squatters' movement and extreme-right movement in the Netherlands that disengagement and the collective decline were predominantly due to non-ideological factors, such as organizational failure and changes in practical circumstances.

Disengagement requires appropriate discursive frames. First, the new disengagement frame must be developed through internal dialogue and reflection among members within the organization, as well as between the organization and the movement, what is called 'social interaction'.[21] Second, for the new disengagement frame to have traction in the movement, credible and influential leaders need to be involved in the process. In the context of violent Islamist movements, rightful leaders are those who are seen by followers and members as pious, theologically knowledgeable and preferably have a history of 'struggle' that could cast legitimacy on the deradicalization process.[22] For this process to be enabled, there must thus be sufficient 'network linkages' between elites and followers and other networks in the movement to communicate the new disengagement frame. This is difficult in a charged political environment that destabilizes these relations.

Another component in successful disengagement frames is the significance of narrative fidelity. In the context of Northern Ireland, it was found that for the new disengagement to be successful, it cannot deviate substantially from the mobilizing frame and attitudes within society.[23] Social and political movements are required to carve out spaces in their narratives that allow them to recalibrate their direction subtly and sensitively while reconciling the goals of the movement with non-violent methods. Below are listed three different types of conditional narratives frames:[24]

1. **Temporal conditionality:** a militant group may delegitimize violence occurring today, but legitimize the past use of violence by the same movement (as with the Provisional Irish Republican Army);
2. **Spatial conditionality:** a militant group may delegitimize violence in Saudi Arabia or the UK, but legitimize it in Syria or Palestine;
3. **Intersectional conditionality:** there is a shift in the type of movement's violence legitimized (e.g. from the Postcolonial Wave to Leftist Wave), but the actor may still legitimize distant violence (e.g. glorifying historical battles), or the actor may shift to legitimizing state violence (e.g. from Irgun/Stern Gang to Israel).

Drawing on the idea that the impact of internal dialogue within the movement acts as a 'domino effect', these disengagement frames can spread to others in the group, to individuals in the movement and the next generation within the movement.[25] But to reiterate, the 'domino effect' of the disengagement process is led by the organization's leadership and occurs between the leadership and group members and between the group and the wider social and political movement. It does not take place between outsiders or state officials, and civil society representatives and isolated individuals disconnected and detached from the violent extremist milieu. Such factors as the presence of social interaction within the movement, the role of credible leaders leading it and the significance of narrative frames that change subtly whilst maintaining fidelity with the movements trigger the 'domino effect' of disengagement.

Another way of understanding this is to view the disengagement process as relational (not entirely individualized), dynamic (not static or fixed), interactive (multifaceted flows of information and dialogue), taking place at multiple levels (not just at the individual level) and contingent on the political state of play. This conception of the fluid and complex process of disengagement is utilized by studies of contentious politics. For example, analysis suggests how political violence ends within the dynamic relational interplay between socio-political context (macro-level), organization dynamics (meso-level) and individual motivations (micro-level). Comparing the Irish Republican Army (IRA) and Red Brigade's transition from armed struggle to non-violence, their approach contextualizes the emergence and decline of political violence within the process of political contestation shaped by relational dynamics involving various political actors. Disengagement, according to their approach, is a highly contextualized and contingent process that cannot generate prescriptive or even universal policies.

This relational model of disengagement is echoed in a study examining the transition of armed violent groups to non-violence in eight countries (Nepal, Egypt, Palestine, West Papua, East Timor, Colombia, Mexico and Western Sahara). The importance of internal and relational/environmental factors which underpin the decision-making process of violent groups was identified. It demonstrates that the factors of transition from armed violence to non-violence occur at multiple levels of analysis. Specifically, for the relationship within groups, between the group and society, the group and the state and the group and the international environment, there are mechanisms of change interacting with each other. For example, this involves a change of leadership and a pragmatic re-evaluation of the goals and means of insurgency to the search for new local or international allies and the cross-border emulation or diffusion of new repertoires of action.[26]

The absence of politics from deradicalization

The primary weakness of current deradicalization interventions is the glaring omission of politics and political reconciliation and negotiation required at the macro-level in making comprehensive and substantial disengagement more likely. Historically, the transition of VE groups and movements to non-violence occurs primarily through political negotiations and mechanisms enabling political justice. In other words, groups stop using political violence when they are encouraged to re-engage in the political process. One study conveys that in the past fifty years, 83 per cent of terrorist campaigns end in one of two ways; terrorist groups are bought into the political fold or they are terminated by action.[27] Of the two, facilitation into politics was the principal way that terrorist campaigns come to an end.

History is replete with famous and celebrated figures who were previously categorized as terrorists but who later went on to become statesmen and heads of state, for example, Nelson Mandela, Yassir Arafat and Gerry Adams. This underscores not only the contested and politicized nature of labelling but also emphasizes how the relationship between the state and non-state violent extremist groups is characterized by dynamic political contestation. In many cases, the major source of grievance fuelling non-state political violence pertains to governance. The emergence of Islamic State post-2014 was a response to the disenfranchisement of Sunnis and the disintegration of the Iraqi state following the invasion of Iraq in 2003. Islamic State was a political project aiming to create a home for Sunnis based on an anti-Westphalian template. State action against particular groups and movements with highly politicized identities have historically precipitated the turn to political violence for the oppressed group. Modern terrorist campaigns, at heart, be it in its provenance or its end, are primarily political.

Campaigns that end or groups that cease to exist do so for many reasons, but, as noted above, they transpire primarily when they are bought into the political fold. This is because the political process orchestrated between state and non-state armed groups enables grievances to be addressed. If the political issues are not entirely mitigated, least the zeitgeist and the political process moves the winds of change in the direction of the recognition and restitution of grievances. In the examples of African National Congress in South Africa, Fatah in Palestine and the IRA in Northern Ireland, it was not that terrorism had proven to work. On the contrary, political dialogue and attempts at reconciliation presided during moments of organizational weakness. It bought to the fore the power of political justice, on the one hand, over and against the practice of retributive justice, on the other hand, where the former concerns itself with the future instead of the past and on reconciliation instead of attribution of blame, and where the latter focuses on punishing individuals and perpetrators for past mistakes and where violence becomes part of the solution. And while the examples above are places where tension and problems remain, and where political justice has not been realized as hoped, they do not suffer from the same levels of violence as before.

While disengaging and reintegrating violent extremist individuals is a worthwhile objective, particularly in the post-criminal space, and is likely to continue to grow and develop, it should nevertheless be seen more in terms of a palliative measure (the equivalence to covering the cracks on one's wall with sticky tape). The current focus on individuals rather than groups, movements and psychology rather than local and global politics may or may not reduce the risk of terrorism. Engaging with at-risk individuals or militants to dislodge their commitment to violence without addressing their political grievances is unlikely to dent the terrorist campaign, even if the social movement that continues to operate and mobilize is cohesive and organized, and where a strong collective insurgent consciousness remains. It is not, in other words, the individual process that is important. Perhaps more significantly for the viability of deradicalization interventions, what is more important is the inclusion of social and political factors into programming the considerations for which, particularly concerning the political grievance, remain ignored by the paradigm of CVE. The importance of politics in supporting or weakening the work of CVE is surveyed in the following chapter, which explores the peculiar realities of contemporary VE, and the central imperative of polarized grievances.

12

Driven to hate

Throughout the 2010s, radical Islamists and far-right extremists in Western Europe carried out numerous terrorist attacks. In March 2019, a self-proclaimed white supremacist of Australian origin murdered fifty-one people in two mosques in the city of Christchurch in New Zealand. Inspired by the likes of Anders Breivik, Brenton Tarrant live-streamed his attack on worshippers gathered for Friday prayers for the world to see. As the fallout from the shootings became ever more pronounced after reflection, analysis and discussion, it is clear that several significant matters are important to state in light of what is known now but was unknown at the moment of the horrific attacks on that fateful Friday afternoon. While attacks such as this are of considerable interest on their own, they do not occur in a vacuum. This chapter explores the geopolitical contexts of the present climate that provide succour, not just to far-right extremists but also radical jihadis. In attempts to introduce viable deradicalization interventions that make a difference to the realities of the lives of people, the importance of the political and cultural context is evident. This is especially the case in the global north, which remains of genuine concern in the light of growing populism, authoritarianism and nativism characterize the profiles of influential nations such as the United States and the United Kingdom, and continue into the post-President Trump and post-Brexit period.

In any sociological analysis of the causes of extremism and radicalization, it is now a matter of fact that the background of the individual requires primary scrutiny. In exploring patterns of socialization, identity formation, as well as issues relating to alienation and exclusion, it is necessary to get into the mind of an individual to assess the development of an ideological perspective that leads them to pursue acts of horrendous violence in the name of some greater cause. One has to come to terms with the fact that, in the case of the Christchurch shooter, he was a self-identified white supremacist who viewed the world in Manichean terms, regarding Islam and Muslims as an ideology and its people who are not simply a blot on the landscape but deserve to be depopulated. This is because they somehow present a risk to the survival of the white nation itself. However, there is rarely any perspective on the nature of this whiteness; that is, its internal diversity or the historical legacies of class formation, colonialism, orientalism, eugenicism or white nationalism that have contributed to defining much of the space occupied by whiteness. A palpable fear is presented about the 'other', whose motivations are to seemingly take over through population expansion. At the same time, there is a decrying of these 'others' for their primitive, backward and hateful natures, thus seemingly legitimizing ethnic nationalism and white supremacism.

Many would regard this as a reality of Islamophobia.[1] They would be accurate in this instance. Islamophobia is not simply a response to a sense of cultural dilution at the hands of some regressive other. It extends into notions of ethnic cleansing of Muslim groups. There is much to expand on the nature of the motivations of the Christchurch attacks, which align with the activities of other individual actors acting on their own. All have carried out an act of ultra-violence in the name of defending against the loss of privileges associated with whiteness at one level, but also the fear of being overtaken by hordes of so-called primitives, on the other. These ideas have motivated far-right extremists in the last few years in several places in the global north, including in Norway, Canada, England and now in New Zealand. The reasons for these are individual, structural, cultural and political.

White men at war

Over the last two decades, in particular, men have perceived considerable challenges to their positions in society, especially in the labour market and education.[2] This is the result of the improving positions of women in these settings but because globalization means that the average young white man has to compete far harder than ever, and where his privileged urban post-industrial patriarchy can no longer be sustained in the light of an increasingly interdependent world. The rage against the loss of power results in the venting of a certain fury against these now-significant others. There was a time, leading up to the events of 9/11, where multiculturalism and diversity were seen as assets that contributed to the well-being of nations, and differences among people were seen to lead to an enriched lived reality that benefits all in the pursuit of human values. But multiculturalism has now become distorted, as the political and media classes began to shift attention away from such notions to a projected association with the risks of polarization, radicalization and terrorism. The social experiment with diversity was stifled before it could be fully applied, which has led to further polarization between groups, with entrenchment in various physical concentrations, in particular, urban spaces. Multiculturalism is not dead in reality but thinkers on the right would regard it so, especially in wanting to emphasize that it is Muslim groups who killed it off.[3]

As social scientists explore the nature of downward social mobility, housing policies and gateways that limit access to certain forms of accommodation as explanatory factors leading to patterns of residential clustering, certain opinion-makers and political voices argue that this outcome is an example of self-styled segregation.[4] This falsehood and misdirection ignores history, past public policy and ongoing patterns of socio-economic inequalities. Moreover, the question of politics has become far more pervasive than ever. Populism, nativism and ethnic nationalism go hand-in-hand as a ruse to mask the failures of domestic policy and the ongoing interventions in faraway lands in pursuit of some greater foreign policy objective that routinely leads to catastrophe and destabilization in those spaces as the norm. In the pursuit of attention-grabbing headlines, sensationalist messaging presented as newsworthy due to the bold ideological motivations of certain press barons on the right of the political spectrum, Islam and Muslims are demonized on such an extensive basis that for it to be Islamophobic is for it to be normal. It takes a critical perspective to distance oneself from the utterances of politicians and some media outlets, but for the less thinking individual, such words are seen as truth.

The attacks in Christchurch were not the result of a random mental health victim on a rampage. They were calculated, cold and clinical. The assailant had a clear agenda – as he identified himself in his writings. He aimed to sow fear and discord by broadcasting his actions all over the world. He alluded to Eurocentric heroism, which borders on ethnic cleansing. The air, thick with Islamophobia, gave him the licence he felt he could legitimately mobilize into political violence and terrorism. Dominant sympathetic voices embolden some, while radicalizing others. And, thus, the circle is complete. It is not always the case that far-right extremists take a pilgrimage of sorts before they are somehow radicalized, turning their newfound ideological perspectives into weaponized political violence and terrorism. The case of the New Zealand shooter appears to be unusual in this regard. There is a real chance that he was radicalized during his travels, although his radicalization was significantly enhanced online.

Undoubtedly, his references to the siege of Vienna by the Ottomans in particular appeal to a certain anti-Muslim sentiment, the latter with contemporary connotations, namely the war in Bosnia. Extremists find in this region the memory of the Ottoman Empire, which held power for 650 years, during which time it was able to annex territories in today's Balkans, South-East Europe, the Caucuses, North Africa and across the Middle East. But in many of the areas of Middle Europe today, these

Ottomans are seen by some as invaders who pillaged villages and raped women. With growing Islamophobia across the world today, these anti-Islam and anti-Muslim voices grow louder at a time when politicians in Hungary, Slovakia, Slovenia and Poland evoke nativist sentiment. Many of these countries were directly affected by the Syrian refugee crisis that began in 2015, and which saw over half a million people walking through the Balkans on their way to countries such as Germany.

A part of the far right in Europe does focus on the historical dynamics of Ottoman history and Christian Europe. For example, Anders Breivik made clear links, seeing himself as a Knight Templar, saving Christianity from the invasive Muslim 'other'.[5] These notions appeal to young men who are at the fringes of their societies, burying themselves in the discourses of the far and radical right online, with its focus on hate towards differences, women and groups with diverse sexual preferences or leanings. It supports the projected inherited importance of the average white male who has to club together for the greater cause to (a) save the 'white nation' from 'invasion' through immigration and mixing and to (b) eliminate these 'other' undesirables as they are breeding at excessive rates. Unless checked they will fully absorb the 'white nation'. There is a tragic absence of historical, political or social depth to these perspectives, which are ideologically instrumentalized to create a 'race war'. The likes of Breivik and the New Zealand, as white supremacists, want a reaction to their terrorism that starts this 'race war'.

Islamophobia and radicalization

There are numerous challenges facing societies in the global north as they grapple with issues of diversity, belonging and mobility, especially when it is apparent that the pernicious forces of race, racism and racialization continue to affect the nature of the lived experience. These concerns are especially pointed when it comes to discussing the experiences of British Muslim minorities, now numbering over three million and making up 5 per cent of the population, and where over 90 per cent of British Muslims live in England, with London containing nearly two-thirds of all Muslims in Britain. These Muslims make up over one-third of all ethnic and racial minorities. One in four of Britain's minorities are South Asian Muslims, and these groups are the focus for much of the gaze of media and political actors interested in questions of cultural relativism, 'grooming', radicalization, extremism and political violence. This disproportional focus, however, takes attention away from the needs and wants of minorities as a whole, concentrating on the negative traits relating to the experiences of the few who fall through fissures created by the workings of society.

Post-war migration processes have led to around two million Bangladeshis, Indians and Pakistanis, with half under the age of twenty-five and one-in-three under the age of fifteen.[6] While these demographics represent particular challenges to participation and engagement, there are concerns around the role of transnationalism. In particular, there are questions of Islam and how it is taken up by groups, what shape it forms in practice and the gaps that remain in terms of questions of religious and secular education for life in a country that is the birthplace of over half of all Muslims in Britain. Transnationalism permits the reproduction of norms and values associated with the old home within the new home, some of which is open to adaptation in the light of interaction and engagement with secular and liberal spaces. But there are other elements of group characteristics that have remained resistant to change. These include aspects of transnational marriages, recreating the challenges of integration afresh generation upon generation. While the current trends suggest that groups are shifting from these practices, they continue to afflict the lives of young people who are compelled to maintain a traditional South Asian heritage bubble existence. Meanwhile the education system in Britain is unable to prepare young people for a diverse, interdependent, mutually enhancing globe in which all have a stake. Rather, it continues to divide along class, racial and ethnic lines.[7]

In this milieu, there are genuine issues of identity, which have implications for belonging and citizenship. There are also concerns relating to gender to consider, including questions relating to masculinity and femininity, as expressed culturally, theologically and politically. How Muslim groups interpret and apply Islam is crucial to understand, with instances of both progressive and regressive readings of the faith leading to risks concerning extremism, radicalization and political violence. These issues reflect on the failures of integration and diversity policy combined with downward pressures on social mobility. It exposes the failures of government policy, leading to the failing of Muslim communities to plan, invest and deliver the Islamic, cultural and civic education and development needs of the younger generations. It reflects on aspects of the most visible and residentially concentrated British Muslims who maintain certain theological, scriptural and cultural norms, unable to educate the younger generations on questions of adaptation to society while adopting a certain Muslimness in the public sphere. While this is not the norm by any stretch, the margins of these spaces reveal acute contestations over being, becoming and belonging.

As a result of these specifically localized problems concerning the unassimilability of Muslims in parts of towns and cities across the country, where these rough edges of Muslimness are regarded as a threating menace but also a potential danger to the rest of society, Islamophobia brews. It does so exponentially, given the problems of growing economic inequality, political division and social conflict that afflict all in an age of anger due to a distrust of the political classes and fear of the 'other' exploited by the same demagogues aiming to capitalize on the discord. Ignorant of history, their frustrations know no bounds due to the lack of any clear vision or direction on the way forward except to retreat into exceptionalism, nativism and populism. The consequences of structural, institutional and cultural Islamophobia, therefore, push some people inwards leading to cultural withdrawal. In some cases, it leads to a few to reject society and the religio-cultural norms of their parents in pursuit of political resistance based on notions of purity or utopianism, some of which lead to paths of VE. In these complex multi-layered realms, violence is seen as a solution to historical, immediate and future predicaments sustained by enmity towards Islam. And thus the circle is complete. At the fringes of society, Islamophobia causes radicalization, and vice versa.

Numerous far right groups play on the dread of Islam, not Muslims, which is a simplistic, unenlightened world view they have come to appreciate. It feeds into and draws sustenance from this Islamophobia, radicalized to the extent of delegitimizing Muslim practices, and the the idea of Islam itself. It creates further tensions, as by nature it engulfs all Muslims, leading to retreat for some who might have ordinarily worked towards balancing Muslim life with a secular existence in liberal democracies. The menacing effects of Islamophobia reflect on wide-ranging aspects of racism, which has the consequence of pushing many more Muslims from all walks of life, although ordinarily still struggling over their Muslimness, to radicalize.

The counter-terror state strikes back

Speaking at a press conference on Sunday where the death of the Islamic State group leader Abu Bakr al-Baghdadi in late October 2019, former US President Donald Trump threatened to 'drop' captured Islamic State fighters on the UK border if Britain does not start repatriating them from Syrian camps. 'They came from France, they came from Germany, they came from the UK. They came from a lot of countries,' he added. 'And I actually said to them, if you [various Western European governments] don't take them, I'm going to drop them right on your border and you can have fun capturing them again.' Earlier that month, US forces removed Alexanda Kotey and El Shafee Elsheikh, part of a group of Islamic State members known as 'The Beatles', from a camp in northern Syria. The aim was to prevent their escape from captivity, but also to potentially take them to Guantanamo Bay. Amid pressure, the UK government decided to bring home children born to British citizens who were part of Islamic State after the debacle concerning Shamima Begum, one of the three surviving teenagers who left their homes in the East End of London to travel to Iraq and Syria.

Londoners Kotey and Elsheikh were radicalized in their twenties and their alleged Islamic State crimes are some of the most heinous imaginable. But little is understood about how they came to be transformed into unhinged executioners. Much has to do with psychological processes that began once they arrived in Syria, although it is accepted that young men such as these join radical Islamist groups due to a combination of individual, structural and ideological convictions. Yet, the socio-economic issues behind their motivations are often overlooked, as is the wider political and cultural fabric of the societies in which they are born and raised, and in which they face systematic patterns of racism, disadvantage and exclusion. During its zenith, Islamic State informed potential recruits that they were not welcome in Britain, but living in Iraq or Syria would solve all of their woes.[8] Through a widespread campaign of information dissemination and ideological communication, young people from marginal society responded to the call. Accounts of anti-Muslim hate rang particularly true for the vulnerable people that Islamic State targeted. Approximately 900 Britons made it to Iraq and Syria. The 'Prevent' strategy has been in place informally since 2003 and formally since 2006, but despite efforts to put up an engaging front, the policy remains controversial.[9] There is a direct relationship between the social outcomes endured by young Muslims in urban areas across Britain and the degree to which they sympathize with violent Islamism.[10]

The social problems facing British Muslims are aggravated by the utterances of populist figures. Islamophobia grows when political actors seek to gain capital from their contempt. Sentiments from US President Donald Trump, which inspired the 'send her back' chant about a critical Muslim congresswoman, Ilhan Omar, created huge damage, as did UK Prime Minister Boris Johnson's suggestion that Muslim women donning the niqab look like 'letterboxes or bank robbers'. Such views embolden elements of the far right, who come to believe that their perspectives have legitimacy. These groups grow due to the same set of structural challenges encountered by British Muslims but also because of the message they hear in the media and politics. In a climate of fear, hostility and intolerance reinforced by polarizing politics and economics, there is a process of reciprocal radicalization, boosted by nativism. It has the effect of normalizing Islamophobic attacks, which are predominantly directed towards visible Muslim women. The high rates of unemployment, poor health, limited housing and relative educational underachievement faced by many are ignored. The fact that half of British Muslims live in the poorest 20 per cent of areas in the country is disregarded. Structural disadvantage and direct and indirect racism normalized through austerity and Islamophobia are significant social issues that receive scant attention.

Islamophobia, however, is not restricted to social and political life. It infuses policymaking. A vast trust deficit remains between the UK government and British Muslims. This has grown since the 'war on terror', made worse by the fact that the only meaningful terms of engagement the UK government has with British Muslims are through the discourse of extremism and terrorism. In this climate, the UK government has blurred the line between moderate and moderated Muslims. Critics of the dominant policy outlook are sidelined by those who seek to maintain the status quo concerning counter-extremism. It indicates a certain paranoia and pressure to conform to prevailing diktats, and to kowtow to dominant (mis)understandings of Islam and Muslims, both locally and globally.[11]

A focus on social and economic conditions is essential to ensure that all groups can share in the fruits of opportunity and mobility. This would diminish the number of people vulnerable to both Islamist and far-right radicalization. Ideology needs to be addressed, but this would be an easier task with the number of vulnerable people made smaller.

It is incumbent upon community and civil society organizations to maintain their efforts to engage with government and with 'other' communities to break down the walls of misunderstanding, intolerance and bigotry. All of this is entirely logical, but a million miles away from the dominant threads of CT, CVE and counter-extremism policy. To deal with the answers to both Islamophobia and radicalization, there needs to be much better UK government thinking on these urgent issues, but also greater honesty on the part of commissions, think tanks, scholars and activists. To appreciate the triggers facing vulnerable young people, it is important to understand the harsh truths facing groups, especially in the poorer parts of the country. More should be done to remain sensitive to the social and economic realities of life for Western European Muslims.

The final chapter of this book surveys some of the ongoing concerns regarding terrorism, radicalization and deradicalization that linger, and the potential challenges facing the decade ahead.

13

Terror politics

In recent years, attention has been focused on the question of Western European-born Muslims who joined a self-declared caliphate in Iraq and Syria in August 2014. Because of various organized attempts to quash its growth by working with local proxy actors such as the People's Protection Units (YPG), the Islamic State was eventually broken down. But some of the remaining fighters, many of whom were foreign, not just Western European but also from other parts of the Middle East, Central Asia and North Africa, remain scattered all over the region. How do these individuals pose a threat in Western European spaces here today? If so, how does this materialize in reality?

Terrorism is a significant social phenomenon with severe implications for human relations, as well as for policymakers who have to deal with both the fear and the threat of VE. Terrorists use the event – or the propaganda of the deed – to spread, promulgate and communicate a political message with specific aims many of which are to do with ethnic, national or religious motivations. However, while there is a tendency to see these demands in religious or ideological terms, at the heart of their actions there is a political goal – and this motivation intends to affect the political climate but also the public at large. That is, to raise awareness and to perpetuate fear, which potentially places those in political power in a difficult position. The adage that 'we will never negotiate with terrorists' is a line promulgated in Hollywood as a sign of defiance and the idea of remaining unyielding in the face of head-on challenges. However, the reality is that numerous behind-the-scenes back channels exist to formulate solutions. For example, the Northern Ireland peace process that publically began in the early 1990s. There is also a situation, for example, in Sri Lanka, when rather than negotiate with the Tamil Tigers, the state did everything possible to eliminate them.

Unquestionably, terrorism is international, as it includes issues of recruitment, training, mobilization and communication. There are also the intellectuals behind the operations who represent the organization and the realization behind the motivations. Foot soldiers are the individuals who act as the frontline of operations, including suicide bombing, as well as other tactics. There are numerous tactics open to terrorists; various kinds of explosive devices can be planted into the ground or even sent through the mail. Anthrax was sent to US parliamentarians in the immediate aftermath of 9/11. In 1994, sarin gas was used by the Aum Shinrikyo doomsday cult in a Tokyo underground to target ordinary commuters. In 1972, after the tragedy of Munich, when Palestinian hijackers held all the members of the Israeli Olympic team, numerous people were killed or injured, including all of the penetrators. While the UN wished to come together to agree on a definition of terrorism, nations from the Middle East, Africa and parts of Asia were reluctant to define terrorism at the time. The main reason was that these nations objected to the classification because it particularizes the Palestinian cause as separate from Israeli state terrorism, Israeli occupation and Israeli laws that discriminate against Palestinians in all walks of life. Thus, a legitimate struggle on the part of the Palestinians could not be seen to be reduced to a notion of terrorism, which was seen as unfair and unreasonable given the significance of state terrorism on the part of the state of Israel.

A few weeks before the events of 9/11, the UN accepted a universal definition of terrorism. It concentrated on ideological and political justification and focused on events and implications. In 2010, another attempt was made by the UN to determine a universal definition of the concept. However, parties could not agree. Thus, a situation occurs in which active use of a particular concept, with all the implications that it raises for policy, practice and perceptions of communities and by others within their domains functions without an agreed or internationally accepted definition. It raises all sorts of implications, because while governments, media and political actors agree on the need to fight terrorism, the balancing of the needs and wants of a liberal, secular and democratic society has to compete with the challenges of potentially introducing authoritarian anti-terrorism-CT measures that are likely to take away freedoms and liberties for all. This definitional problem affects criminalizing terrorism, especially when terrorism does not see borders.

The politics of terror

When it comes to the political process, there are various dimensions to consider. Fear is a political tool, an opportunity in the hands of state actors in pursuit of attempts to limit terrorism. After the attacks in the Bataclan, France initiated a state of emergency that was rolled over month after month. Similarly, after the failed coup events of July 2016, Turkey introduced emergency rule, which temporarily abolished the constitution, allowing President Recep Tayyip Erdoğan to introduce sanctions against a suspected terrorist organization. This included defining the category of terrorism in a way to include groups who may have been tangentially associated with a large social movement, and all without external checks or internal balances. As a result, hundreds of thousands of people were targeted by biased repressive state practices in the immediate aftermath of the failed coup events. Soon after the events of 9/11, the United States initiated a response led by the Republicans to go after Saddam Hussein, falsely accusing him of collaborating with Osama bin Laden. These actions were grounded in the idea of a predetermined approach to the Middle East, specifically in relation to Iraq, which was the target of a bombing campaign during the last few months of the second President Clinton administration in 1998, while the Monica Lewinsky affair writ large in the public consciousness.

It was the second President Bush administration that coined the term 'war on terror', which was arguably a public relations opportunity in the wake of the events of 9/11, cementing the ideals of the neoconservative movement within the Republican Party and notions of a New American Century. President Obama dropped the term 'war on terror' after he came into power in 2008 soon after British Foreign Office officially acknowledged that it would stop using the term from 2007 onwards. Laws introduced during times of particular moral panics concerning terrorism are often more about enhancing state power and authority. The resultant impact on actual patterns of CT policy and practice in being able to eliminate the threat of terrorism is often a distant reality. In many ways, terrorism is the opportunity for states take actions that they would rather not have to, but these actions are not always aimed at solutions to immediate problems or their longer historical narratives, but indeed to ratchet up a response that is seemingly hard-hitting and therefore politically impactful. It could be argued, therefore, that Osama bin Laden has been the most successful terrorist in history. Governments are able to use measures in response to terrorism as a way in which to potentially demonize, marginalize and ostracized an entire group whose internal variations to ethnicity, language, religious practice or even socio-economic positions become irrelevant unless they can be instrumentalized. This can be seen with the vilification presented towards particular Muslim minorities, leading to accusations of Islamophobia and institutional racism, which, unsurprisingly, has a role in motivating disaffected young angry Muslim minorities across Western Europe, sending them into the theatres of war far away from their countries of birth. They exercise what they regard as legitimate violence based on real-world experiences, predicated an out-of-this-world eschatology, which also acts as a tool in the redemption of this-world sinners.

The emergence of the Guantánamo Bay detention camp in Cuba generated huge public outcry across the world. However, the camp remains open, although the number of prisoners has been dramatically reduced over the years. The dehumanization, use of psychological tactics to break down the will of individuals and the use of certain techniques of interviewing and questioning led to severe questions being asked of the Bush administration. Although President Obama promised to disband Guantanamo Bay, he was unable to effect that change. While there are policy, political and legal issues to grapple with, there is also the matter of media. As the maxim goes, 'if it bleeds, it leads'. The question of media manufacturing sensationalist news as an opportunity to improve sales is not unknown, but coverage for particular stories also reflects the ideological bias of senior editors, even if individual journalists have more independent minds. In general, the use of the word 'terrorist' in media reporting is often wide-ranging, from the deployment of terms such as 'economic terrorism', 'eco-terrorism', 'cyber terrorism', 'home-grown terrorism' and even other concepts such as a 'lone wolf' or a 'lone actor'. All have particular uses but also carry with them the ability of media outlets to concentrate on the individual, personality and circumstantial factors related to the radicalization processes, but omit the structural, ideological and political motivations, specifically when it comes to home-grown Anglo-Saxon terrorism in the global north. On the other hand, Muslims are routinely implicated in preparing, plotting or attempting to initiate an act of terrorism, with the immediate reaction being to focus on the networks associated with the religious and political ideology, where these networks are said to be real and significant. In the case of 'lone actor' terrorists, there are undoubtedly networks that are at play, but there is often a virtual network too, one that acts as an echo chamber for the fomentation of ideological reconfiguration and intensification.

In this perspective, it is easy to forget one other group in this schematic. That is the terrorists themselves. They would rarely call themselves terrorists but such terms as a 'martyr', 'freedom fighter' or 'revolutionary'. These groups see their actions as a legitimate struggle against oppressive internal and external threats that seem to delegitimize the group's identity, norms and values in the context of a position as a minority or to do with ongoing internal or external colonization. Moreover, while a great deal of the terrorism lens in the last few decades has been on the jihadi variation, left-leaning, right-leaning, animal welfare, anti-abortion or for any other group that seeks to use VE to achieve a political or ideological awareness or objective, are also important features in this regard, especially in the United States. In recent periods, Western Europe has seen a rise in far-right VE radicalization and terrorism. It can be reasonably stated that there are reciprocal forms of cumulative extremism, which are largely to do with actors who find near identical reasons to hate each other, mirroring each other's justification, rationalization and objectives.

Terrorism studies is a complex and murky field, which leads to interdisciplinary and multidisciplinary methodological approaches, specifically from the social sciences. There is less a focus on the philosophy of terrorism than there is on the psychology of terrorism, or the sociology, which explores the background, the context of historical processes and the complexity of social relations that need to be better understood to better understand where these gaps are enough to create VE, and in some cases, terrorism. While there is a great deal of emphasis placed on the notion that something needs to be done to prevent terrorism and introduce CVE measures, the solutions do not always appreciate deeper understanding.

The foreign fighter peril

Unsurprisingly, while there is great attention placed on the returnee foreign fighters of Muslim origin, the phenomenon is neither new nor does it have an especially Islamic flavour. There has been a movement to the Middle East in recent periods, but foreign fighters have been on the move at all times, circulating from one struggle to the next, from one cause to the next, from one place to the next. While there are groups operating in particular localized struggles, the reality is that foreign fighters are far more deadly and far more successful in their campaigns. At one level, a transnational relationship is a reason motivating people to mobilize from their country of birth, often as minorities, to a different country to engage in an ideological struggle that motivates them to expect to potentially give up their lives in its pursuit.[1] But the fact of the transnational link is insufficient, as it says nothing about their agency, the direction of flow or the practicalities of the process. Suggesting that it may be caused by transnationalism is insufficient in explaining why many choose not to go, yet face the same challenges over their identities but not to the extent of engaging with a struggle elsewhere. Some are prepared to risk their lives and others may not. Yet they both share the same ideological concerns around their group identity being under threat at the hands of an external or internal agitator.

This is a weak argument but popular because it focuses on identity and group formations and takes attention away from historical, social and political circumstances that created the conditions for instability, conflict and VE. In many ways, it makes complete sense to argue that transnational identities play a role in motivation and recruitment, but it says nothing specifically about this relationship beyond stating the obvious. The real question is why many more choose not to, and for those that do go, how are particular individual circumstances driving their narratives beyond that of the group, which is then instrumentalized for individual gains? Because this theory is conceptually straightforward to understand, its plausibility provides it greater salience. As the group's identity is under threat, it reaches out to others, some of whom are elsewhere. Some are willing to accept the narrative of the group under threat as one in which they sympathize with, motivating some to help facilitate its militarization by supporting the supplies of arms, as Lord Byron did for the Greek forces fighting a war of independence against the Ottomans in the 1820s. Byron was prompted by the idea of preserving some notion of historical antiquity through the protection of Greek culture and civilization in his own time.

In the 1980s, the Jammu Kashmir Liberation Front was able to motivate young British Pakistanis from the inner cities of Birmingham to join the struggle to support Kashmiris facing occupation by Indian forces. Later, these foreign fighters returned to England under the radar of the security services. Some later joined the Afghan struggle against the Soviets in the late 1980s, which the British government took a softer line towards, allowing individuals to freely return. In the first instance, the oppressor was seen as the foreign Indian state due to rising Hindutva that seeks to erase the Muslim memory from India, for example, by changing names of towns to their original Sanskrit. In recent periods, populism, authoritarianism and anti-Muslimism have gone hand in hand in India. The idea of supporting a religio-nationalist struggle against India transformed into a battle against the perceived attack on Islam by communism in Afghanistan. Abdullah Azzam was the Palestinian with Muslim Brotherhood sympathies who had arrived in Peshawar in 1984, a few years into the Soviet invasion. Frustrated at why so few came to join the efforts, he began a concerted campaign to draw into the theatre of war Muslims from all over the world, specifically the Middle East, Central Asia and North Africa. It is through this calling that Osama bin Laden found his way into Afghanistan by the end of the 1980s. Given his vast fortune and his growing ideological ambitions, he was able to bankroll much of the initial post-Soviet jihad, that is, until he was ostracized by his family in Saudi Arabia. It is here that Azzam began to write openly, vehemently expressing to others the view that Afghanistan was the beginning of a global struggle against those who would seek to suppress Muslim nations and the Islamic faith. However, much of this narrative was sustained, supported logistically and operationalized by foreign intelligence agencies such as the CIA that wished to encourage a dedicated fighting force against the struggle, thereby keeping American or other Western troops off the ground as much as possible. But when the Soviets were defeated, some of the countries from which these foreign fighters originated refused to have them back.

These well-trained, battle-hardened, ideologically aroused warriors had no other fight to fight. Until the mid-1990s, Afghanistan was in a bitter civil war, largely between north and south. But by 1995, along came a group called the Taliban, which means 'the students' in Pashto. They were mobilized to prevent the raping, killing, assassinations and tribal rivalries ripping the Afghans apart. However, as they took power, their motives were seized by others. When Osama bin Laden returned, more ideologically motivated now that Saudi Arabia had prevented him from remaining in his country of birth, the Taliban became a force on their own. And it is out of the caves of Afghanistan that a plot was hatched to take down America's most symbolic and iconic buildings, namely the World Trade Center, the Pentagon and the White House on the same day. Failing first in 1993, Osama bin Laden was successful in 2001. In between these years, many of fighters moved to Bosnia to war against the Serbs, and then returned to Afghanistan towards the end of the 1990s.[2]

'Islamofascism'

Many of these foreign fighters are of Muslim origin and, therefore, the immediate question raised is whether there is something specific about being Muslim and foreign fighter that is separate from other categorization. The concept of the Muslim Ummah is a powerful narrative, but this is unsurprising and unremarkable because these kinds of religious ties have existed between Muslims across the world since the beginning of Islam. What is peculiar about this emergence of the Muslim foreign fighter relates more to contemporary developments to communication technologies, issues relating to social alienation and inequality in the new countries as diaspora groups, and the effects of globalization upon determining a narrative concerning a post-9/11 'war on terror' that is perceived as a war on Islam and Muslim countries. Globalization and transnationalism have weakened or fractured national identities of the host nation as well as of those groups who have migrated and chosen to live in their new home as citizens of the state but then continue to face various conflicts over identity formations that are subject to various transformations within the sending regions themselves. At the same time, the forces of Wahhabism, which is the central, highly hierarchical, financially equipped, political, ideological and religious approach to a radical Sunni Islam that seeks to return to a more literal interpretation of the early years relating to the formation of Islam aim to do away with innovations (bidaa) entered the domain of global Islam. It is highly significant that sixteen out of the nineteen hijackers who flew into those prominent symbolic sites in the United States on 9/11 were of Saudi origin, with many having been trained in the training camps of Afghanistan.

When President George W. Bush talked about 'Islamofascism', he was referring ideological perspectives that emanate from Saudi Arabia and other Gulf states. Saudi Arabia has invested significantly in rebranding its national image, including in promoting the idea of a progressive vision of growth and development in a region in the wane because of global oil pricing. The House of Saud continues to promulgate a narrow vision of Sunni Islam, which can lead to all sorts of ideological, political and violent outcomes due to protagonists seemingly protecting the essence and purity of the religion as seen through Wahhabism. It is interesting that these foreign fighters travel to different parts of the periphery of Islam to reshape the Islamic experience in these areas, but have little to add to their domestic situations. In the case of Abdullah Azzam, he never returned to Palestine and in the case of Osama bin Laden, he was banned from his country of birth, Saudi Arabia. Meanwhile, of the political structures in these countries are weak, creating the conditions for lingering authoritarianism. This violent global Islamism is an offshoot of pan-Islamism that emerged in the 1970s, with its centre in Saudi Arabia. It paints external enemies with even greater vigour than in the past, funnelling money into local chapters, even in the diaspora, through charities and funds. As these pan-Islamists reached Afghanistan in the mid-1980s, it started a wave of Muslim foreign fighter activity that continues to this day. The hiking of oil prices in 1974 made funding these endeavours easier.[3] Although the theory of a centralized radicalizing force is appealing, it takes out of the equation the role played by the United States and other Western powers in arming, training, mobilizing and instrumentalizing these groups – in recent period but also historically, for example concerning the First World War (2.5 million Muslims fought for France, the British Empire and Russia) – where a certain form of jihad was evoked to mobilize groups.[4]

Throughout Western Europe, the current threat level over returning foreign fighters from Islamic States remains high, although most of those who are returning to their home countries after the collapse of Islamic State are women and children. It is curious to note that approximately one-third of the people who went from the Netherlands were white convert women (around 100 of 300). And it appears that of the 160 or so who are still in Iraq/Syria, half of them are indeed Dutch women, with a significant proportion who converted. This is also the case concerning those who came from Belgium, Germany and the UK – that is, the disproportional number of women converts who ended up in Iraq and Syria. This is an important question that has not been fully answered. Are these native-born Western Europeans seeking something that has been denied to them in their countries of birth? Or are parts of the ideology the central driving force?.

Concluding thoughts

This book has come a long way from initially exploring terrorism, its origins in a historical and political context, and the implications of state terrorism, especially in the Middle East and elsewhere in the world. The nature of Islamic political radicalism, in particular concerning Muslim minorities experience in Western Europe, has been discussed.

In considering genocide and the abuse of human rights, another level of state terrorism is explored. In assessing the nature of CT policy and practice, one is invariably facing all sorts of challenges of ensuring the balance between maintaining liberty and freedom while safeguarding national security, and that adequate measures are in place to protect, pursue, prepare and prevent further terrorist attacks against the civilian population or public institutions and infrastructure. It is important to bring together some of these themes and to address the question of where one goes from here in thinking through what terrorism means in the 2020s. The implications for communities, institutions and policymakers are also contemplated, including how societies are affected by acts of terrorism and CT policy. One is also looking at how society breaks down, leading to gaps and fissures through which vulnerable individuals, majority and minority, find themselves on a path towards redemption, self-realization and self-awareness, where group membership and the identities associated with belonging to the group may encourage some to move from non-violent political radicalization to physical acts of violence that may include terrorism.

Numerous issues arise from the radicalization of vulnerable youths and the repercussions raised for securitization, policing and intelligence, in particular, in the online space. But while a role for the internet in radicalization exists, the precise nature of the processes that entice young people and 'activate' their radicalization requires greater understanding.[5] Nor is it possible to argue that the internet increases the rate or intensity of terrorism, as many studies show it as a facilitator.[6] Furthermore, the offline world is an important element, despite the power of the internet to connect people and ideas. Importantly, the situation of young people who might be susceptible to radicalization emerges within a particular social, cultural and political context. Indeed, the restructuring of the economic base, from manufacturing to services, has resulted in a 'left behind' generation of marginalized, disenfranchised, alienated young men (and women), both indigenous and minority. In Western Europe, the growth of far-right and Islamist extremism is directly associated with transformations to economy and society that have resulted in groups feeling unable to contribute to their existence, leading to alienation and anomie. In this context, anger and resentment are directed against the perceived 'other'. For far-right groups, theirs is a 'counter-jihad' narrative that instrumentalizes the rhetoric of ethnic nationalism, anti-immigration and anti-religion, namely a concentration on anti-Islam.[7] In addition to politicizing groups, this online far-right online is an alternative reality that serves individuals seeking to activate their political views but also provides information on how to make bombs. Individuals can remain reclusive and undetected in an arena where aggressive gaming is an issue; permitting people such as Anders Breivik and Brenton Tarrant to transform from a hardcore gamer to a terrorist.[8] In the case of radical Islamists, they project their frustration at a global level, where a sense of obligation to a self-transcendental cause is the defining characteristic. However, while anger surfaces in many young people, only a few depart from the view that their group identity is under threat to actual instances of VE. The online world is a space for the exploration of identities of the 'self' and the 'other' and questions of being *and* becoming.

In thinking through the future of terrorism, there are several important scenarios to consider. Terrorism today reflects notions of social and ethnic conflict in societies all over the world, but the role of the state in promulgating a certain form of state terrorism is often underreported. The current focus has been on Islamic political radicalism and, in more recent periods, the emergence of far-right extremism, which has largely come about as a response to issues of diversity, multiculturalism and the negative perceptions of Islam and Muslims in the West. There are also alliances made with conspiracy theory movements such as QAnon that raise new risks to society. While it is possible to deter online radicalization when regarded as a specific threat, social media industries are in the hands of private capital, who enjoy the business of making profits, even out of social and political conflicts. Moreover, as legislation tightens to ensure that ordinary civilians are under greater surveillance to prevent any development from soft to hard radicalization. It generates implications for freedoms in a liberal democracy. There is also the question of research. How neighbourhood and local area post-industrial social contents impact on identities, intergenerational change and questions of adaptation to the changing nature of the economy are fundamentally important concerns in research. The problems of extremism and radicalization are local area in nature and, therefore, the solutions are local in nature too. The idea of a centralized, top-down, universalist approach to dealing with terrorism that CVE thinking often aims to do can stigmatize many committees on the fringes of integration, adaptation and attempts at social mobility. With downward social pressures, the problems of social exclusion lead to a sense of underachievement. Many are unable to challenge the disadvantages head-on, a few slip into VE and even fewer into terrorism.

In many ways, terrorism can never be eliminated because terrorism reflects the changing nature of societies and political struggles experienced by particular individuals and groups. Terrorists are averse to technology. The online space offers more opportunity than ever to radicalize, incentivize and mobilize vulnerable people into extremism, radicalization and terrorism. Both state and non-state actors are culpable in this. The lives of ordinary people are being affected by polarization, tribalism and identity politics. These issues will remain important as the 2020s unfold and as societies fragment further into camps that have differential access to opportunity, power and influence. The efforts made by CVE scholars and practitioners will remain under the microscope for the foreseeable future.

Notes

Chapter 1

1 Abbas, Tahir and Hamid, Sadek (eds) (2019) *Political Muslims: Understanding Youth Resistance in a Global Context*, New York: Syracuse University Press.
2 Abbas, Tahir (2019) *Islamophobia and Radicalisation: A Vicious Cycle*, London and New York: Hurst and Oxford University Press.
3 Pippa Norris, Montague Kern and Marion Just (eds) (2003) *Framing Terrorism: The News Media, the Government and the Public*, London and New York: Routledge.
4 Hoffman, Bruce (1998) *Inside Terrorism*, New York: Columbia University Press, p. 1.
5 Ibid., p. 3.
6 Garrison, Arthur H. (2007) 'Defining Terrorism: Philosophy of the Bomb, Propaganda by Deed and Change through Fear and Violence', *Criminal Justice Studies* 17(4): 259–79.
7 The events of 7/7 (July 2005 London Tube and bus bombings) killed 52 and injured 784 in 2005. A year earlier, in 2004, 191 Spaniards were killed in ten simultaneous bomb attacks in Madrid.
8 Hoffman, op. cit., p. 12.
9 Ibid., p. 16.
10 Schmid, Alex P. (2010) 'Frameworks For Conceptualising Terrorism', *Terrorism and Political Violence* 16(2): 197–221.
11 Jackson, Richard, Smyth, Marie Breen and Gunning, Jeroen (eds) (2009) *Critical Terrorism Studies: A New Research Agenda*, London and New York: Routledge.

Chapter 2

1 Jackson, Richard (2008) 'The Ghosts of State Terror: Knowledge, Politics and Terrorism Studies', *Critical Studies on Terrorism* 1(3): 377–92, p. 377.

2   Foucault, Michel (1980) *Power/Knowledge: Selected Interviews and Other Writings 1972–1977*, New York: Pantheon.
3   Jackson, op. cit., p. 380.
4   Ibid., p. 385.
5   Ibid., p. 388.
6   Ibid.
7   Tucker, David (2001) 'What Is New about the New Terrorism and How Dangerous Is It?' *Terrorism and Political Violence* 13(3): 1–14.
8   Pappé, Ilan (2006) *The Ethnic Cleansing of Palestine*, Oxford: Oneworld.
9   Kapitan, Tomis (2004) 'State Terrorism and Counter-Terrorism', in Igor Primoratz (ed.) *Terrorism: The Philosophical Issues*, Basingstoke: Palgrave Macmillan, pp. 175–91, p. 177.
10 Ibid., 179.
11 Ibid., 180.
12 Ibid., 184.
13 Blakeley, Ruth (2009) *State Terrorism and Neoliberalism: The North in the South*, Abingdon: Routledge, p. 27.
14 Jäckle, Sebastian and Baumann, Marcel (2017) '"New Terrorism" = Higher Brutality? An Empirical Test of the "Brutalization Thesis"', *Terrorism and Political Violence* 29(5): 875–901, p. 875.

Chapter 3

1   Ragazzi, Francesco (2017) 'Countering Terrorism and Radicalisation: Securitising Social Policy?' *Critical Social Policy* 37(2): 163–79, p. 163; Younis, Tarek and Jadhav, Sushrut (2019) 'Islamophobia in the National Health Service: An Ethnography of Institutional Racism in PREVENT's Counter-Radicalisation Policy', *Sociology of Health & Illness* 42(3): 610–26, iFirst, pp. 1–17.
2   Enders, Walters and Sandler, Todd (2005) 'After 9/11: Is It All Different Now?', *Journal of Conflict Resolution* 49(2): 259–77, p. 260.
3   Jackson, Richard, Smyth, Marie Breen and Gunning, Jeroen (eds) (2009) *Critical Terrorism Studies: A New Research Agenda*, London and New York: Routledge.

4   Jackson, Richard (2005) *Writing the War on Terrorism: Language, Politics and Counter-Terrorism*, Manchester: Manchester University Press, p. 9.
5   Jackson et al., op cit.
6   Field, Anthony (2017) 'The Dynamics of Terrorism and Counterterrorism: Understanding the Domestic Security Dilemma', *Studies in Conflict & Terrorism* 40(6): 470–83.
7   Sedgwick, Mark (2010) 'The Concept of Radicalization as a Source of Confusion', *Terrorism and Political Violence* 22(4): 479–94.
8   Wolfendale, Jessica (2007) 'Terrorism, Security, and the Threat of Counterterrorism', *Studies in Conflict and Terrorism* 30(1): 75–92.
9   Primoratz, Igor (2002) 'State Terrorism and Counter-Terrorism', in Igor Primoratz (ed.) *Terrorism: The Philosophical Issues*, Basingstoke: Palgrave Macmillan, pp. 113–27.
10 Byman, Daniel (2013) 'Why Drones Work: The Case for Washington's Weapon of Choice', Foreign Affairs, July/August, p. 32.
11 Della Porta, Donatella (2018) 'Radicalization: A Relational Perspective', *Annual Review of Political Science* 21: 461–74.
12 Burke, Jason (2003) *Al-Qaeda*, London and New York: Penguin.
13 Rogers, Paul (2013) 'Lost Cause: Consequences and Implications of the War on Terror', *Critical Studies on Terrorism* 6(1): 13–28, p. 20.
14 Espinoza, Marina (2018) 'State Terrorism: Orientalism and the Drone Programme', *Critical Studies on Terrorism* 11(2): 376–93.
15 Ibid., p. 390.
16 McCrisken, Trevor (2011) 'Ten Years On: Obama's War on Terrorism in Rhetoric and Practice', *International Affairs* 87(4): 781–801.

Chapter 4

1   Boghossian, Paul (2010) 'The Concept of Genocide', *Journal of Genocide Research* 12(1–2): 69–80.
2   United Nations (1948) *Convention on the Prevention and Punishment of the Crime of Genocide* (no. 1021).
3   Figueroa Ibarra, Carlos (2013) 'Genocide and State Terrorism in Guatemala, 1954–1996: An Interpretation', *Bulletin of Latin American Research* 32(s1): 151–73.

4   Abed, Mohammed (2015) 'The Concept of Genocide Reconsidered', *Social Theory and Practice* 41(2): 328–56.
5   Feierstein, Daniel (2014) *Genocide as Social Practice*, New York: Rutgers University Press.
6   Barrington, Lowell W. (1997) '"Nation" and "Nationalism": The Misuse of Key Concepts in Political Science', *PS: Political Science and Politics* 30(4): 712–16.
7   Gagnon, V.P., Jr. (1994) 'Ethnic Nationalism and International Conflict: The Case of Serbia', *International Security* 19(3): 130–66, p. 131.
8   Stone, Dan (2004) 'The Historiography of Genocide: Beyond "Uniqueness" and Ethnic Competition', *Rethinking History* 8(1): 127–42.
9   Weitz, Eric D. (2015) *A Century of Genocide: Utopias of Race and Nation*, Princeton, NJ: Princeton University Press, p. 9.
10 Behrens, Paul, Terry, Nicholas and Jensen, Olaf (2017) (eds) *Holocaust and Genocide Denial: A Contextual Perspective*, Abingdon: Routledge.
11 Sekulić, Duško (2007) 'Ethnic Cleansing', in George Ritzer (ed.) *The Blackwell Encyclopedia of Sociology*, Oxford: Wiley, pp. 1450–2.
12 Besançon, Marie L. (2005) 'Relative Resources: Inequality in Ethnic Wars, Revolutions, and Genocides', *Journal of Peace Research* 42(4): 393–415.
13 Anderson, Benedict (1983) *Imagined Communities: Reflections on the Origin and Spread of Nationalism*, London and New York: Verso.
14 Ther, Philipp (2016) *The Dark Side of Nation-States: Ethnic Cleansing in Modern Europe*, New York and Oxford: Berghahn.
15 Hiebert, Maureen S. (2017) *Constructing Genocide and Mass Violence: Society, Crisis, Identity*, Abingdon: Routledge, p. 10.
16 Jones, Adam (2006) *Genocide: A Comprehensive Introduction*, Abingdon: Routledge.
17 Ankit, Rakesh (2016) *The Kashmir Conflict: From Empire to the Cold War, 1945–66*, Abingdon: Routledge, p. 9.
18 Ibid., p. 10.
19 Chatta, Illays (2009) 'Terrible Fate: "Ethnic Cleansing" of Jammu Muslims in 1947', *Journal of Pakistan Vision* 10(1): 117–40, p. 118.
20 Khan, Waheeda and Majumdar, Sramana (2000) 'Qualitative Exploration of Salient Incidents of Violence Exposure among Youth in Kashmir: Beyond Direct Violence', in M. Seedat et al. (eds) *Enlarging the Scope of*

Peace Psychology, Springer International, NL: Peace Psychology Book Series, pp. 39–54, p. 41.
21. Bhat, Fayaz Ahmad and Mathur, P.K. (2017) 'Education and Employment among Muslims in Indian Jammu and Kashmir', *Journal of Muslim Minority Affairs* 37(1): 94–113.
22. Ibid.
23. Dench, Bette (1994) 'Dismembering Yugoslavia: Nationalist Ideologies and the Symbolic Revival of Genocide', *American Ethnologist* 21(2): 367–90.
24. Leydesdorff, Selma (2011) *Surviving the Bosnian Genocide: The Women of Srebrenica Speak*, Bloomington: Indiana University Press.
25. Jacobs, Janet (2017) 'The Memorial at Srebrenica: Gender and the Social Meanings of Collective Memory in Bosnia-Herzegovina', *Memory Studies* 10(4): 423–9, p. 425.
26. Article 3 of the Constitution of the Union of Myanmar, 2008 (listing national groups). See also Amnesty International (2017) *Caged without a Roof*, London: Amnesty International.
27. Ibid., p. 20.
28. United Nations Human Rights Council (2018) *Report of the Independent International Fact-Finding Mission on Myanmar* A/HRC/39/64, New York: UN, paragraph 89, p. 17.
29. Zarni, Maung and Cowley, Alice (2014) 'The Slow-Burning Genocide of Myanmar's Rohingya', *Pacific Rim Law and Policy Journal Association* 23(3): 683–754, p. 685.

Chapter 5

1. Abbas, Tahir (2011) *Islamic Radicalism and Multicultural Politics: The British Experience*, London and New York: Routledge.
2. US Agency for International Development (2011) *The Development Response to Violent Extremism and Insurgency: Putting Principles into Practice*, Washington, DC: USAID.
3. United Nations General Assembly (2015) *Plan of Action to Prevent Violent Extremism*, New York: UNGA A/70/674.

4 Bennhold, Katrin (2015) 'Young Medics Were Lured by Briton to Join ISIS', *New York Times*, 17 July.
5 Neumann, Peter (2008) 'Introduction', in P.R. Neumann (ed.) *Perspectives on Radicalisation and Political Violence – Papers from the First International Conference on Radicalisation and Political Violence*, London: Kings College International Centre for the Study of Radicalisation and Political Violence, pp. 3–7.
6 Canadian Security Intelligence Services (2018) *Mobilisation to Violence (Terrorism) Research*, Ottawa: Government of Ottawa Intelligence Assessment Branch, pp. 4–5.
7 Ibid., p. 6.
8 Schuurman, Bart and Eijkman, Quirine (2015) 'Indicators of Terrorist Intent and Capability: Tools for Threat Assessment', *Dynamics of Asymmetric Conflict* 8(3): 215–31.
9 Sedgwick, Mark (2010) 'The Concept of Radicalisation as a Source of Confusion', *Terrorism and Political Violence* 22(4): 479–94.
10 Sageman, Mark (2004) *Understanding Terror Network*, Philadelphia: University of Pennsylvania Press.
11 Neumann, Peter and Rogers, Brooke (2007) *Recruitment and Mobilisation for the Islamist Militant Movement in Europe*, London: Kings College International Centre for the Study of Radicalisation and Political Violence, p. 11.
12 Wikström, Per-Olof H and Bouhana, Noémie (2017) 'Analyzing Radicalization and Terrorism: A Situational Action Theory', in G. LaFree and J.D. Freilich (eds) *The Handbook of the Criminology of Terrorism*, Oxford: Wiley Blackwell, pp. 175–86.
13 Day, Joel and Kleinmann, Scott (2017) 'Combating the Cult of ISIS: A Social Approach to Countering Violent Extremism', *The Review of Faith and International Affairs* 15(3): 14–23.
14 Della Porta, Donatella (2013) *Clandestine Political Violence*. New York: Cambridge University Press.

Chapter 6

1 USAID (2009) *Guide to the Drivers of Violent Extremism*, Washington, DC: United States Agency for International Development, pp. 65–6.

2. Sageman, Marc (2008) 'A Strategy for Fighting International Islamist Terrorists', *The ANNALS of the American Academy of Political and Social Science* 618(1): 223–31.
3. Atran, Scott (2010) *Talking to the Enemy: Violent Extremism, Sacred Values, and What It Means to Be Human*, London: Penguin.
4. Venhaus, John (2010), *Why Youth Join al-Qaeda*, Washington, DC: United States Institute of Peace, p. 8.
5. Borum, Randy (2014) 'Psychological Vulnerabilities and Propensities for Involvement in Violent Extremism', *Behavioral Sciences and the Law* 32(3): 286–305.
6. Giddens, Anthony (1991) *Modernity and Self-Identity: Self and Society in the Late Modern Age*, Stanford, CA: Stanford University Press.
7. Atran, Scott (2016) 'The Devoted Actor: Unconditional Commitment and Intractable Conflict Across Cultures', *Current Anthropology* 57(13): 192–203.
8. Borum, Randy, op. cit., p. 293.
9. Taylor, Charles (1994) *Multiculturalism and the Politics of Recognition*, Princeton, NJ: Princeton University Press.
10. Based on Maslow, Abraham H. (1954) *Motivation and Personality*, New York: Harper and Row.
11. Weinstein, Jeremy M. (2005) 'Resources and the Information Problem in Rebel Recruitment', *Journal of Conflict Resolution* 49(4): 598–624.
12. Gurr, Ted R. (1970) *Why Men Rebel*, Princeton, NJ: Princeton University Press.
13. Özerdem, Alpaslan and Podder, Sukanya (2011) 'Disarming Youth Combatants: Mitigating Youth Radicalization and Violent Extremism', *Journal of Strategic Security* 4(4): 63–80, p. 66.
14. Wiktorowicz, Quinton (2005) *Radical Islam Rising: Muslim Extremism in the West*, London and New York: Rowman and Littlefield.
15. Maher, Shiraz (2016) *Salafi-Jihadism: The History of an Idea*, London and New York: Hurst and Oxford University Press.
16. Raffie, Dina Al (2013) 'Social Identity Theory for Investigating Islamic Extremism in the Diaspora', *Journal of Strategic Security* 6(4): 67–91.
17. Ibid., p. 90.
18. Moghaddam, Fathali M. (2005) 'The Staircase to Terrorism: A Psychological Exploration', *American Psychologist* 60(2): 161–9, p. 168.

19 Webber, David and Kruglanski, Arie W. (2018) 'The Social Psychological Makings of a Terrorist', *Current Opinion in Psychology* 19: 131–4.
20 Decker, Scott H. and Pyrooz, David C. (2015) '"I'm down for a Jihad" How 100 Years of Gang Research Can Inform the Study of Terrorism, Radicalization and Extremism', *Perspectives on Terrorism* 9(1): 104–12.
21 Webber and Kruglanski, op. cit., p. 132.
22 Ibid.
23 Jasko, Katarzyna Jasko, LaFree, Gary and Kruglansk, Arie (2016) 'Quest for Significance and Violent Extremism: The Case of Domestic Radicalization', *Political Psychology* 38(5): 815–31.
24 Elden, Stuart (2007) 'There Is a Politics of Space Because Space Is Political: Henri Lefebvre and the Production of Space', *Radical Philosophy Review* 10(2): 101–16.
25 Johnson, Peter (2013) 'The Geographies of Heterotopia', *Geography Compass* 7(11): 790–803.
26 Eatwell, Roger (2006) 'Community Cohesion and Cumulative Extremism', *The Political Quarterly* 77(2): 204–16.
27 Ebner, Julia (2017) *The Rage: The Vicious Circle of Islamist and Far-Right Extremism*, London and New York: I.B. Tauris.

Chapter 7

1 Wagner, Markus and Meyer, Thomas M. (2016) 'The Radical Right as Niche Parties? The Ideological Landscape of Party Systems in Western Europe, 1980–2014', *Political Studies* 65(1S): 84–107.
2 Lee, Martin A. (1999) *The Beast Reawakens: Fascism's Resurgence from Hitler's Spymasters to Today's Neo-Nazi Groups and Right-Wing Extremists*. London: Routledge.
3 Rzepnikowska, Alina (2019) 'Racism and Xenophobia Experienced by Polish Migrants in the UK before and after Brexit Vote', *Journal of Ethnic and Migration Studies* 45(1): 61–7.
4 Archer, Toby (2013) 'Breivik's Mindset: The Counterjihad and the New Transatlantic Anti-Muslim Right', in Taylor, M., Currie, P.M. and Holbrook, D. (eds) *Extreme Right-Wing Political Violence and Terrorism* (London: Bloomsbury, 2013), pp. 169–86.

5   Koehler, Daniel (2016) 'Right-Wing Extremism and Terrorism in Europe: Current Developments and Issues for the Future', *Prism: A Journal of the Center for Complex Operations* 4(2): 84–104.
6   Pratt, Douglas (2015) 'Islamophobia as Reactive Co-radicalization', *Islam and Christian–Muslim Relations* 26(2): 205–18.
7   Feldman, M. (2015) *From Radical-Right Islamophobia to 'Cumulative Extremism'*, London: Faith Matters.
8   Busher, Joel (2017) 'Why Even Misleading Identity Claims Matter: The Evolution of the English Defence League', *Political Studies* 66(2): 323–38.
9   Hafez, Farid (2014) 'Shifting Borders: Islamophobia as Common Ground for Building Pan-European Right-Wing Unity', *Patterns of Prejudice* 48(5): 479–99.
10 Bangstad, Sindre (2014) *Anders Breivik and the Rise of Islamophobia*, London and New York: Zed.
11 Bartlett, Jamie and Birdwell, Jonathon (2013) *Cumulative Radicalisation between the Far-Right and Islamist Groups in the UK: A Review of Evidence*, London: Demos; Ebner, Julia (2017) *The Rage: The Vicious Circle of Islamist and Far-Right Extremism*, London and New York: I.B. Tauris.
12 Pisoiu, Daniela (2015) 'Subcultural Theory Applied to Jihadi and Right-Wing Radicalization in Germany', *Terrorism and Political Violence* 27(1): 9–28.
13 Peach, Ceri (1994) 'The Meaning of Segregation', *Planning Practice and Research* 11(2): 137–50.
14 Saull, Richard (2015) 'Capitalism, Crisis and the Far-Right in the Neoliberal Era', *Journal of International Relations and Development* 18(1): 25–51.
15 Global Research (2017) 'Non-Muslims Carried Out More Than 90% of All Terrorist Attacks in America', http://www.globalresearch.ca/non-muslims-carried-out-more-than-90-of-all-terrorist-attacks-in-america/5333619. Accessed 16 February 2017.
16 Jones, Seth G. (2018) *The Rise of Far-Right Extremism in the United States*, Washington, DC: Center for Strategic and International Studies Brief's (November).
17 McDowell, Linda (2000) 'The Trouble with Men? Young People, Gender Transformations and the Crisis of Masculinity', *International Journal of Urban and Regional Research* 24(1): 201–09.

18 Uhlmann, Milena (2008) 'European Converts to Terrorism', *Middle East Quarterly* 15(3): 31–7.
19 Papadopoulos, Linda (2010) *Sexualisation of Young People: Review*, London: Home Office.
20 Foucault, Michel (2004) *The Birth of Biopolitics*, Basingstoke: Palgrave Macmillan.
21 Furlow, R.B. and Goodall, H.L. (2011) 'The War of Ideas and the Battle of Narratives: A Comparison of Extremist Storytelling Structures', *Cultural Studies ↔ Critical Methodologies* 11(3): 215–23.
22 Kaplan, Jeffry, Lööw, Heléne and Malkki, Leena (2014) 'Introduction to the Special Issue on Lone Wolf and Autonomous Cell Terrorism', *Terrorism and Political Violence* 26(1): 1–12.
23 Bailey, Gavin and Edwards, Phil (2016) 'Rethinking "Radicalisation": Microradicalisations and Reciprocal Radicalisation as an Intertwined Process', *Journal for Deradicalisation* 12: 255–81.
24 Borum, Randy (2011) 'Radicalization into Violent Extremism I: A Review of Social Science Theories', *Journal of Strategic Security* 4(4): 7–36.
25 Alam, Yunis and Husband, Charles (2013) 'Islamophobia, Community Cohesion and Counter-Terrorism Policies in Britain', *Patterns of Prejudice* 47(3): 235–52.

Chapter 8

1 Abbas, Tahir (2017) 'Ethnicity and Politics in Contextualising Far Right and Islamist Extremism', *Perspectives on Terrorism* 11(3): 54–61.
2 Koehler, Daniel (2016) *Right-Wing Terrorism in the 21st Century: The 'National Socialist Underground' and the History of Terror from the Far-Right in Germany*, Abingdon: Routledge, p. 88.
3 NCTV (2018) *Fluctuating Waves of Right-Wing Extremist Violence in Western Europe*, The Hague: Ministry of Justice and Security.
4 Eatwell, Roger (2006) '*Community Cohesion and Cumulative Extremism in Contemporary Britain'*, *The Political Quarterly* 77(2): 204–2016, p. 213.
5 Busher, Joel and Macklin, Graham (2015) 'Interpreting "Cumulative Extremism": Six Proposals for Enhancing Conceptual Clarity', *Terrorism and Political Violence* 27(5): 884–905, p. 892.

6 Kallis, Aristotle, Zeiger, Sara and Öztürk, Bilgehan (eds) (2018) *Violent Radicalisation and Far-Right Extremism in Europe*, Ankara, Turkey: Foundation for Political, Economic and Social Research.
7 Koehler (2016), op. cit., p. 89.
8 Schmid, Alex, P. (2013) *Radicalisation, De-radicalisation, Counter-Radicalisation: A Conceptual Discussion and Literature Review*, The Hague: The International Centre for Counter-Terrorism.
9 Sumpter, Cameron (2017) 'Countering Violent Extremism in Indonesia: Priorities, Practice and the Role of Civil Society', *Journal of Deradicalisation* 11: 112–47.
10 Bailey and Edwards 'Rethinking "Radicalisation"', 255–81.
11 Knott, Kim, Lee Benjamin and Copeland, Simon (2018) *Briefings: Reciprocal Radicalisation – Full Report*, Lancaster University: Centre for Research and Evidence on Security Threats.
12 Schmid (2013), op. cit.
13 Holbrook, Donald (2013) 'Far Right and Islamist Extremist Discourses: Shifting Patterns of Enmity', in M. Taylor, P.M. Currie, and D. Holbrook (eds) *Extreme Right Wing Political Violence and Terrorism*, New York: Bloomsbury Academic, pp. 215–37, p. 216.
14 Knott, Lee and Copeland (2018), op. cit.
15 Bouhana, Noémie, Corner, Emily, Gill, Paul and Schuurman, Bart (2018) 'Background and Preparatory Behaviours of Right-Wing Extremist Lone Actors: A Comparative Study', *Perspectives on Terrorism* 12(6): 150–63.
16 Knott, Lee and Copeland (2018), op. cit., p. 5.
17 Bouhana et al. (2018), op. cit., p. 158.
18 Busher and Macklin (2015), op. cit.
19 Gaston, Sophie (2017) *Briefing Paper: Far-Right Extremism in the Populist Age*, London: Demos.
20 TE-SAT (2018) *European Union Terrorist Situation and Trend Report*, The Hague: EUROPOL.
21 Bouhana et al. (2018).
22 Koehler (2016), op. cit., p. 96.
23 TE-SAT (2018).
24 Almohammad, Asad (2018) 'From Total Islam to the Islamic State: Radicalization Leading to Violence Dynamics as a Subject of Reciprocal Affordance Opportunities', *Journal for Deradicalisation* 15: 1–42.

25 NCTV (2018), p. 8.
26 Ibid.
27 Ibid., p. 12.
28 Ibid.
29 NCTV (2018), p. 17.
30 Goodwin, Matthew (2013) *The Roots of Extremism: The English Defence League and the Counter-Jihad Challenge*, London: Chatham House, p. 3.
31 Ibid., p. 6.
32 Holbrook (2013), op. cit., p. 233.
33 Ibid.
34 Sumpter (2017), op. cit.
35 NCTV (2018), p. 18.
36 Pisoiu, Daniela and Ahmed, Reem (2016) 'Capitalizing on Fear: The Rise of Right-Wing Populist Movements in Western Europe', in Institute for Peace Research and Security Policy at the University of Hamburg (ed.) *OSCE Yearbook 2015*, Baden-Baden: Germany, pp. 165–76, p. 170.
37 Goodwin (2013), op. cit., p. 5.
38 Meeteren, Masja and Oostendorp, Linda (2018) 'Are Muslims in the Netherlands Constructed as a "Suspect Community"? An Analysis of Dutch Political Discourse on Terrorism in 2004–2015', *Crime, Law and Social Change* 71(5): 525–40.
39 Sterkenburg, Nikki, Gssime, Yasmine and Meines, Marije (2019) *Local-Level Management of Far-Right Extremism*, Rotterdam: Radicalisation Awareness Network.
40 Melzer, Ralf and Serafin, Sebastian (2013) *Right-Wing Extremism in Europe*, Berlin: Friedrich-Ebert-Stiftung, p. 30.
41 Gaston (2017), op. cit., p. 5.
42 Ibid.
43 Goodwin (2013), op. cit., p. 4.
44 Pantazis, Christina and Pemberton, Simon (2009) 'From the "Old" to the "New" Suspect Community: Examining the Impacts of Recent UK Counter-Terrorist Legislation', *British Journal of Criminology* 49(5): 646–66.
45 Kallis et al. (2018), p. 14.
46 Ibid.
47 Gaston (2017), op. cit., p. 7.

48   Sterkenburg et al., p. 9.
49   Kallis et al. (2018), p. 33.
50   Ibid., p. 17.
51   Vellenga, Sipco and Groot Kees de (2019) 'Securitization, Islamic Chaplaincy, and the Issue of (De)radicalization of Muslim Detainees in Dutch Prisons', *Social Compass* 66(2): 224–37, p. 231.
52   Sterkenburg et al. (2019), p. 9.
53   Ibid.

Chapter 9

1   Abbas, Tahir and Awan, Imran (2015) 'Limits of UK Counterterrorism Policy and Its Implications for Islamophobia and Far Right Extremism', *International Journal for Crime, Justice and Social Democracy* 4(3): 16–29.
2   Coppock, Vicki and McGovern, Mark (2014) '"Dangerous Minds"? Deconstructing Counterterrorism Discourse, Radicalisation and the "Psychological Vulnerability" of Muslim Children and Young People in Britain', *Children Society* 28(3): 242–56.
3   Blackbourn, Jessie and Walker, Clive (2016) 'Interdiction and Indoctrination: The Counter-Terrorism and Security Act 2015', *Modern Law Review* 79(5): 840–70.
4   Young, Jock (1999) *The Exclusive Society: Social Exclusion, Crime and Difference in Late Modernity*, London: Sage.
5   Dekeseredy, Walter S. and Schwartz, Martin D. (2010) 'Friedman Economic Policies, Social Exclusion, and Crime: Toward a Gendered Left Realist Subcultural Theory', *Crime Law and Social Change* 54(2): 159–70.
6   Vidino, Lorenzo, Marone, Francesco and Entenmann, Eva (2017) *Fear Thy Neighbor: Radicalization and Jihadist Attacks in the West*. Leiden: George Washington University's Program on Extremism, The Hague: The Italian Institute for International Political Studies and the International Centre for Counter-Terrorism.
7   Archer, Toby (2009) 'Welcome to the Umma: The British State and Its Muslim Citizens since 9/11', *Cooperation and Conflict* 44(3): 329–47.
8   Edwards, Phil (2016) 'Closure through Resilience: The Case of Prevent', *Studies in Conflict and Terrorism* 39(4): 292–307.

9 Heath-Kelly, Charlotte (2017) 'The Geography of Pre-criminal Space: Epidemiological of Radicalisation Risk in the UK Prevent Strategy, 2007–2017', *Critical Studies on Terrorism* 10(2): 297–319.
10 Lewis, Hannah and Craig, Gary (2014) '"Multiculturalism Is Never Talked About": Community Cohesion and Local Policy Contradictions in England', *Policy and Politics* 42(1): 21–38.
11 Aistrope, Tim (2016) 'The Muslim Paranoia Narrative in Counter-Radicalisation Policy', *Critical Studies on Terrorism* 9(2): 182–204.
12 Awan, Imran and Zempi, Irene (2016) 'The Affinity between Online and Offline Anti-Muslim Hate Crime: Dynamics and Impacts', *Aggression and Violent Behavior* 27: 1–8.
13 Thomas, Paul (2012) *Responding to the Threat of Violent Extremism: Failing to Prevent*, London: Bloomsbury.
14 Bertelsen, Preben (2015) 'Danish "Prevent"ive Measures and De-Radicalization Strategies: The Aarhus Model', *Panorama: Insights into Asian and European Affairs* 1: 241–53.
15 Ragazzi, Francesco (2016) 'Suspect Community or Suspect Category? The Impact of Counterterrorism as "Policed Multiculturalism"', *Journal of Ethnic and Migration Studies* 42(5): 724–41.
16 Schuurman, Bart, Bakker, Edwin and Eijkman, Quirine (2016) 'Structural Influences on Involvement in European Homegrown Jihadism: A Case Study', *Terrorism and Political Violence* 30(1): 97–115.
17 O'Donnell, Aislinn (2015) 'Securitisation, Counterterrorism and the Silencing of Dissent: The Educational Implications of "Prevent"', *British Journal of Educational Studies* 64(1): 53–76.
18 Qureshi, Asim (2015) '"PREVENT": Creating "Radicals" to Strengthen Anti-Muslim Narratives', *Critical Studies on Terrorism* 8(1): 181–91.
19 Dawson, Lorne L. and Amarasingam, Amarnath (2017) 'Talking to Foreign Fighters: Insights into the Motivations for Hijrah to Syria and Iraq', *Studies in Conflict and Terrorism* 40(3): 191–210.
20 Jarvis, Lee and Lister, Michael (2012) 'Disconnected Citizenship? The Impacts of Anti-terrorism Policy on Citizenship in the UK', *Political Studies* 61(3): 656–75.
21 Spalek, B. (2016) 'Radicalisation, De-radicalisation and Counter-Radicalisation in Relation to Families: Key Challenges for Research, Policy and Practice', *Security Journal* 29(1): 39–52.

22 Institute for Economics and Peace (2019) *Global Terrorism Index 2019: Measuring the Impact of Terrorism*, Sydney: IEP.
23 Altermark, Niklas and Nilsson, Hampus (2018) 'Crafting the "Well-Rounded Citizen": Empowerment and the Government of Counterradicalization', *International Political Sociology* 12(1): 53–69.
24 Lowe, David (2017) '"Prevent" Strategies: The Problems Associated in Defining Extremism – The Case of the UK', *Studies in Conflict and Terrorism* 40(11): 917–33.

Chapter 10

1 Horgan, John and Braddock, Kurt (2010) 'Rehabilitating the Terrorists?: Challenges in Assessing the Effectiveness of De-radicalization Programs', *Terrorism and Political Violence* 22(2): 267–91.
2 Bjørgo, Tore (2009) 'Process of Disengagement from Violent Groups from the Extreme Right', in T. Bjørgo and J Horgan (eds) *Leaving Terrorism Behind*, London and New York: Routledge, pp. 30–48.
3 Horgan, John. (2009) *Walking away from Terrorism: Accounts of Disengagement from Radical and Extremist Movements*, London and New York: Routledge, p. 152.
4 Horgan, John (2008) 'Deradicalization or Disengagement? A Process in Need of Clarity and a Counterterrorism Initiative in Need of Evaluation', *Perspectives on Terrorism* 2(4): 3–8.
5 Veldhuis, Tinka (2012) *Designing Rehabilitation and Reintegration Programmes for Violent Extremist Offenders: A Realist Approach*, The Hague: The International Centre for Counter-Terrorism, p. 2.
6 Barrellea, Kate (2015) 'Pro-integration: Disengagement from and Life after Extremism', *Behavioral Sciences of Terrorism and Political Aggression* 7(2): 129–42, p. 133.
7 Ibid.
8 Marsden, Sarah V. (2017) *Reintegrating Extremists: Deradicalisation and Desistance*, Basingstoke: Palgrave-Pivot.
9 Ibid.
10 Marsden, Sarah V. (2018) '"Deradicalisation" and Desistance: A Framework for Supporting the Reintegration of Extremists', *Lancaster University Centre for Research and Evidence on Security Threats Crest Security Review* 7, pp. 4–5.

11 Fink, Naureen C. and Hearne, Ellie B. (2008) *Beyond Terrorism: Deradicalization and Disengagement from Violent Extremism*, New York: International Peace Institute, p. 16.
12 Schuurman, Bart and Bakker, Edwin (2016) 'Reintegrating Jihadist Extremists: Evaluating a Dutch Initiative, 2013–2014', *Behavioral Sciences of Terrorism and Political Aggression* 8(1): 66–85.
13 Gielen, Amy-Jane (2018) 'Exit Programmes for Female Jihadists: A Proposal for Conducting Realistic Evaluation of the Dutch Approach', *International Sociology* 33(4): 454–72.
14 Horgan, John (2014) *The Psychology of Terrorism*, London and New York: Routledge.
15 El-Said, Hamed and Harrigan, Jane (2012) *Deradicalising Violent Extremists: Counter-Radicalisation and Deradicalisation Programmes and Their Impact in Muslim Majority States*, London and New York: Routledge.
16 Koehler, Daniel (2015) 'De-radicalization and Disengagement as Counter-Terrorism and Prevention Tools. Insights from Field Experiences Regarding German Right-Wing Extremism and Jihadism', M. Lombadri et al. (eds) *Countering Radicalisation and Violent Extremism among Youth to Prevent Terrorism*, Amsterdam: IOS, 120–50.
17 Bjørgo, Tore and Horgan, John (eds) (2009) *Leaving Terrorism Behind*, London and New York: Routledge.
18 Horgan, John (2009) 'Individual Disengagement: A Psychological Analysis', in T. Bjørgo and J. Horgan (eds) *Leaving Terrorism Behind*, London and New York: Routledge, pp. 17–29, pp. 21–2.
19 Ibid., p. 25.
20 Ibid., p. 26
21 Ibid.
22 Bjørgo, Tore (2009), op. cit., pp. 36–40.
23 Barrellea, Kate (2015) op. cit., pp. 134–5.
24 OHCHR (2017) *Guidance to States on Human Rights-Compliant Responses to the Threat Posed by Foreign Fighters*, New York: United Nations Office of the United Nations High Commissioner for Human Rights et al.
25 Berger, J.M. (2016) *Making CVE Work: A Focused Approach Based on Process Disruption*, The Hague: The International Centre for Counter-Terrorism, pp. 16–17.

Chapter 11

1. Farrall, Stephan (2002) *Rethinking What Works with Offenders. Probation, Social Context and Desistance from Crime*, Devon: Willan.
2. Bromley, David G. (1988) *Falling from the Faith: Causes and Consequences of Religious Apostasy*, London: Sage.
3. Hwang, Julie Chernov (2017) 'The Disengagement of Indonesian Jihadists: Understanding the Pathways', *Terrorism and Political Violence* 29(2): 277–95, p. 290.
4. Clubb, Gordon (2016) *Social Movement De-radicalisation and the Decline of Terrorism: The Morphogenesis of the Irish Republican Movement*, London and New York: Routledge.
5. Ibid., p. 21.
6. Lindekilde, Lasse (2012) 'Value for Money? Problems of Impact Assessment of Counter-Radicalization Policies on End Target Groups: The Case of Denmark', *European Journal on Criminal Policy and Research* 18: 385–402.
7. Ibid., p. 394.
8. Schuurman, Bart and Bakker, Edwin (2016) 'Reintegrating Jihadist Extremists: Evaluating a Dutch Initiative, 2013–2014', *Behavioral Sciences of Terrorism and Political Aggression* 8(1): 66–85.
9. Romaniuk, Peter (2015) *Does CVE Work? Lessons Learned from the Global Effort to Counter Violent Extremism*, Washington, DC: Global Center on Cooperative Security, September.
10. Crenshaw, Martha (1991) 'How Terrorism Declines', *Terrorism and Political Violence* 3(1): 69–87.
11. Cronin, Audrey Kurth (2006) 'How Al-Qaida Ends: The Decline and Demise of Terrorist Groups', *International Security* 31(1): 7–48.
12. Ibid., p. 14.
13. Rapoport, David C. (2004) 'The Four Waves of Modern Terrorism', in A.K. Cronin and J.M. Ludes (eds) *Attacking Terrorism: Elements of a Grand Strategy*, Washington, DC: Georgetown University Press, pp. 46–73.
14. Richardson, Louise and Weinberg, Leonard (2003) 'Conflict Theory and the Trajectory of Terrorist Campaigns in Western Europe', in A. Silke (ed.) *Research on Terrorism: Trends, Achievements and Failures*, London: Frank Cass, pp. 138–60.

15 Tucker, Robert C. (1967) 'The Deradicalization of Marxist Movements', *The American Political Science Review* 61(2): 343–58; Demant, Froukje, Slootman, Marike, Buijs, Frank and Tillie, Jean (2008) *Decline and Disengagement: An Analysis of Processes of Deradicalisation*, Amsterdam: International Migration and Ethnic Studies.
16 Tucker (1967), op. cit.
17 Ibid., p. 348.
18 Ibid.
19 Ibid., p. 349.
20 Demant et al. (2008), op. cit., pp. 122–6.
21 Ashour, Omar (2009) *The De-radicalization of Jihadists: Transforming Armed Islamist Movements*, New York and London: Routledge.
22 Ibid., pp. 15–16.
23 Club, Gordon (2016), p. 24.
24 Ibid.
25 Ibid., p. 30.
26 Dudouet, Véronique (2013) 'Dynamics and Factors of Transition from Armed Struggle to Nonviolent Resistance', *Journal of Peace Research* 50(3): 401–13.
27 Jones, Seth and Libicki, Martin (2008) *How Terrorist Groups End. Lessons for Countering Al Qa'ida*, Santa Monica, CA: RAND Corporation, pp. viii–xiv.

Chapter 12

1 Esposito, John L. and Iner, Derya (eds) (2019) *Islamophobia and Radicalization: Breeding Intolerance and Violence*, Basingstoke: Palgrave Macmillan.
2 Kimmel, Michael S. (2018) 'The Contemporary "Crisis" of Masculinity in Historical Perspective', in H. Brod (ed.) *The Making of Masculinities*, London: Routledge.
3 Heath, Anthony and Demireva, Neli (2014) 'Has Multiculturalism Failed in Britain?', *Ethnic and Racial Studies* 37(1): 161–80.
4 Simpson, Ludi (2004) 'Statistics of Racial Segregation: Measures, Evidence and Policy', *Urban Studies* 41(3): 661–81.
5 Bangstad, *Anders Breivik and the Rise of Islamophobia*.

6 Muslim Council of Britain (2015) *British Muslims in Numbers: A Demographic, Socio-Economic and Health Profile of Muslims in Britain Drawing on the 2011 Census*, London: MCB.
7 Bukodi1, Erzsébet, Goldthorpe, John H., Halpin, Brendan and Waller, Lorraine (2016) 'Is Education Now Class Destiny? Class Histories across Three British Birth Cohorts', *European Sociological Review* 32(6): 835–49.
8 Zelin, Aaron Y. (2015) 'Picture or It Didn't Happen: A Snapshot of the Islamic State's Official Media Output', *Perspectives on Terrorism* 9(4): 85–97.
9 CAGE Advocacy (2016) *The 'Science' of Pre-Crime*, London: Cage Advocacy.
10 Berger, Lars (2016) 'Local, National and Global Islam: Religious Guidance and European Muslim Public Opinion on Political Radicalism and Social Conservatism', *West European Politics* 39(2): 205–28.
11 Kundnani, Arun (2014) *The Muslims Are Coming: Islamophobia, Extremism, and the Domestic War on Terror*, London and New York: Verso.

Chapter 13

1 Malet, David (2013) *Foreign Fighters: Transnational Identity in Civil Conflicts*, New York: Oxford University Press.
2 Brachman, Jarret M. (2009) *Global Jihadism: Theory and Practice*, London and New York: Routledge.
3 Hegghammer, Thomas (2010) 'The Rise of Muslim Foreign Fighters: Islam and the Globalization of Jihad', *International Security* 35(3): 53–94.
4 Dreyfuss, Robert (2006) *Devil's Game: How the United States Helped Unleash Fundamentalist Islam*, New York: Metropolitan.
5 Aly, Anne (2016) 'Brothers, Believers, Brave Mujahideen: Focusing Attention on the Audience of Violent Jihadist Preachers', *Studies in Conflict & Terrorism* 40(1): 62–76.
6 Gill, Paul, Corner, Emily, Thornton, Amy and Conway, Maura (2015) *What are the Roles of the Internet in Terrorism? Measuring Online Behaviours of Convicted UK Terrorists*, Brussels: VOX-Pol Network of Excellence.

7 Ford, Robert and Goodwin, Matthew, J. (2014) *Revolt on the Right: Explaining Support for the Radical Right in Britain*, Abingdon: Routledge.
8 Ravndal, Jacob Aasland (2013) 'Anders Behring Breivik's Use of the Internet and Social Media', *JEX Journal for Deradicalization and Democratic Culture* 2: 172–85.

Bibliography

Abbas, Tahir (2011) *Islamic Radicalism and Multicultural Politics: The British Experience*, London and New York: Routledge.

Abbas, Tahir (2017) 'Ethnicity and Politics in Contextualising Far Right and Islamist Extremism', *Perspectives on Terrorism* 11(3): 54–61.

Abbas, Tahir (2019) *Islamophobia and Radicalisation: A Vicious Cycle*, London and New York: Hurst and Oxford University Press.

Abbas, Tahir and Awan, Imran (2015) 'Limits of UK Counterterrorism Policy and Its Implications for Islamophobia and Far Right Extremism', *International Journal for Crime, Justice and Social Democracy* 4(3): 16–29.

Abbas, Tahir and Hamid, Sadek (eds) (2019) *Political Muslims: Understanding Youth Resistance in a Global Context*, New York: Syracuse University Press.

Abed, Mohammed (2015) 'The Concept of Genocide Reconsidered', *Social Theory and Practice* 41(2): 328–56.

Ahsan Ullah, A.K.M. (2016) 'Rohingya Crisis in Myanmar: Seeking Justice for the "Stateless"', *Journal of Contemporary Criminal Justice* 32(3): 285–301.

Aistrope, Tim (2016) 'The Muslim Paranoia Narrative in Counter-Radicalisation Policy', *Critical Studies on Terrorism* 9(2): 182–204.

Alam, Yunis and Husband, Charles (2013) 'Islamophobia, Community Cohesion and Counter-Terrorism Policies in Britain', *Patterns of Prejudice* 47(3): 235–52.

Almohammad, Asad (2018) 'From Total Islam to the Islamic State: Radicalization Leading to Violence Dynamics as a Subject of Reciprocal Affordance Opportunities', *Journal for Deradicalisation* 15: 1–42.

Altermark, Niklas and Nilsson, Hampus (2018) 'Crafting the "Well-Rounded Citizen": Empowerment and the Government of Counterradicalization', *International Political Sociology* 12(1): 53–69.

Amnesty International (2017) *Caged without A Roof*, London: Amnesty International.

Anderson, Benedict (1983) *Imagined Communities: Reflections on the Origin and Spread of Nationalism*, London and New York: Verso.

Ankit, Rakesh (2016) *The Kashmir Conflict: From Empire to the Cold War, 1945–66*, Abingdon: Routledge.

Archer, Toby (2009) 'Welcome to the Umma: The British State and Its Muslim Citizens since 9/11', *Cooperation and Conflict* 44(3): 329–47.

Archer, Toby (2013) 'Breivik's Mindset: The Counterjihad and the New Transatlantic Anti-Muslim Right', in Taylor, M., Currie, P.M. and Holbrook, D. (eds) *Extreme Right-Wing Political Violence and Terrorism*, London: Bloomsbury, pp. 169–86.

Ashour, Omar (2009) *The De-radicalization of Jihadists: Transforming Armed Islamist Movements*, New York and London: Routledge.

Atran, Scott (2010) *Talking to the Enemy: Violent Extremism, Sacred Values, and What It Means to Be Human*, London: Penguin.

Atran, Scott (2016) 'The Devoted Actor: Unconditional Commitment and Intractable Conflict across Cultures', *Current Anthropology* 57(13): 192–203.

Awan, Imran and Zempi, Irene (2016) 'The Affinity between Online and Offline Anti-Muslim Hate Crime: Dynamics and Impacts', *Aggression and Violent Behavior* 27: 1–8.

Bailey, Gavin and Edwards, Phil (2016) 'Rethinking "Radicalisation": Microradicalisations and Reciprocal Radicalisation as an Intertwined Process', *Journal for Deradicalisation* 12: 255–81.

Bangstad, Sindre (2014) *Anders Breivik and the Rise of Islamophobia*, London and New York: Zed.

Barrellea, Kate (2015) 'Pro-integration: Disengagement from and Life after Extremism', *Behavioral Sciences of Terrorism and Political Aggression* 7(2): 129–42.

Barrington, Lowell W. (1997) '"Nation" and "Nationalism": The Misuse of Key Concepts in Political Science', *PS: Political Science and Politics* 30(4): 712–16.

Bartlett, Jamie and Birdwell, Jonathon (2013) *Cumulative Radicalisation between the Far–Right and Islamist Groups in the UK: A Review of Evidence*, London: Demos.

Behrens, Paul, Terry, Nicholas and Jensen, Olaf (2017) (eds) *Holocaust and Genocide Denial: A Contextual Perspective*, Abingdon: Routledge.

Bennhold, Katrin (2015) 'Young Medics Were Lured by Briton to Join ISIS', *New York Times*, 17 July.

Berger, J.M. (2016) *Making CVE Work: A Focused Approach Based on Process Disruption*, The Hague: The International Centre for Counter-Terrorism.

Berger, Lars (2016) 'Local, National and Global Islam: Religious Guidance and European Muslim Public Opinion on Political Radicalism and Social Conservatism', *West European Politics* 39(2): 205–28.

Bertelsen, Preben (2015) 'Danish "Prevent"ive Measures and De-radicalization Strategies: The Aarhus Model', *Panorama: Insights into Asian and European Affairs* 1: 241-53.

Besançon, Marie L. (2005) 'Relative Resources: Inequality in Ethnic Wars, Revolutions, and Genocides', *Journal of Peace Research* 42(4): 393-415.

Bhat, Fayaz Ahmad and Mathur, P.K. (2017) 'Education and Employment among Muslims in Indian Jammu and Kashmir', *Journal of Muslim Minority Affairs* 37(1): 94-113.

Bjørgo, Tore (2009) 'Process of Disengagement from Violent Groups from the Extreme Right', in T. Bjørgo and J Horgan (eds) *Leaving Terrorism Behind*, London and New York: Routledge, pp. 30-48.

Bjørgo, Tore and Horgan, John (eds) (2009) *Leaving Terrorism Behind*, London and New York: Routledge.

Blackbourn, Jessie and Walker, Clive (2016) 'Interdiction and Indoctrination: The Counter-Terrorism and Security Act 2015', *Modern Law Review* 79(5): 840-70.

Blakeley, Ruth (2009) *State Terrorism and Neoliberalism: The North in the South*, Abingdon: Routledge.

Boghossian, Paul (2010) 'The Concept of Genocide', *Journal of Genocide Research* 12(1-2): 69-80.

Borum, Randy (2011) 'Radicalization into Violent Extremism I: A Review of Social Science Theories', *Journal of Strategic Security* 4(4): 7-36.

Borum, Randy (2014) 'Psychological Vulnerabilities and Propensities for Involvement in Violent Extremism', *Behavioral Sciences and the Law* 32(3): 286-305.

Bouhana, Noémie, Corner, Emily, Gill, Paul and Schuurman, Bart (2018) 'Background and Preparatory Behaviours of Right-Wing Extremist Lone Actors: A Comparative Study', *Perspectives on Terrorism* 12(6): 150-63.

Brachman, Jarret M. (2009) *Global Jihadism: Theory and Practice*, London and New York: Routledge.

Bromley, David G. (1988) *Falling from the Faith: Causes and Consequences of Religious Apostasy*, London: Sage.

Bukodi, Erzsébet, Goldthorpe, John H., Halpin, Brendan and Waller, Lorraine (2016) 'Is Education Now Class Destiny? Class Histories across Three British Birth Cohorts', *European Sociological Review* 32(6): 835-49.

Burke, Jason (2003) *Al-Qaeda*, London and New York: Penguin.

Busher, Joel (2017) 'Why Even Misleading Identity Claims Matter: The Evolution of the English Defence League', *Political Studies* 66(2): 323–38.

Busher, Joel and Macklin, Graham (2015) 'Interpreting "Cumulative Extremism": Six Proposals for Enhancing Conceptual Clarity', *Terrorism and Political Violence* 27(5): 884–905.

Byman, Daniel (2013) 'Why Drones Work: The Case for Washington's Weapon of Choice', *Foreign Affairs*, July/August.

CAGE Advocacy (2016) *The 'Science' of Pre-Crime*, London: Cage Advocacy.

Canadian Security Intelligence Services (2018) *Mobilisation to Violence (Terrorism) Research*, Ottawa: Government of Ottawa Intelligence Assessment Branch.

Chatta, Illays (2009) 'Terrible Fate: "Ethnic Cleansing" of Jammu Muslims in 1947', *Journal of Pakistan Vision* 10(1): 117–40.

Clubb, Gordon (2016) *Social Movement De-radicalisation and the Decline of Terrorism: The Morphogenesis of the Irish Republican Movement*, London and New York: Routledge.

Coppock, Vicki and McGovern, Mark (2014) '"Dangerous Minds"? Deconstructing Counterterrorism Discourse, Radicalisation and the "Psychological Vulnerability" of Muslim Children and Young People in Britain', *Children Society* 28(3): 242–56.

Crenshaw, Martha (1991) 'How Terrorism Declines', *Terrorism and Political Violence* 3(1): 69–87.

Cronin, Audrey Kurth (2006) 'How Al-Qaida Ends: The Decline and Demise of Terrorist Groups', *International Security* 31(1): 7–48.

Dawson, Lorne L and Amarasingam, Amarnath (2017) 'Talking to Foreign Fighters: Insights into the Motivations for Hijrah to Syria and Iraq', *Studies in Conflict and Terrorism* 40(3): 191–210.

Day, Joel and Kleinmann, Scott (2017) 'Combating the Cult of ISIS: A Social Approach to Countering Violent Extremism', *The Review of Faith and International Affairs* 15(3): 14–23.

Decker, Scott H. and Pyrooz, David C. (2015) '"I'm Down for a Jihad" How 100 Years of Gang Research Can Inform the Study of Terrorism, Radicalization and Extremism', *Perspectives on Terrorism* 9(1): 104–12.

Dekeseredy, Walter S. and Schwartz, Martin D. (2010) 'Friedman Economic Policies, Social Exclusion, and Crime: Toward a Gendered Left Realist Subcultural Theory', *Crime Law and Social Change* 54(2): 159–70.

Della Porta, Donatella (2013) *Clandestine Political Violence*, New York: Cambridge University Press.

Della Porta, Donatella (2018) 'Radicalization: A Relational Perspective', *Annual Review of Political Science* 21: 461–74.

Demant, Froukje, Slootman, Marike, Buijs, Frank and Tillie, Jean (2008) *Decline and Disengagement: An Analysis of Processes of Deradicalisation*, Amsterdam: International Migration and Ethnic Studies.

Dench, Bette (1994) 'Dismembering Yugoslavia: Nationalist Ideologies and the Symbolic Revival of Genocide', *American Ethnologist* 21(2): 367–90.

Dreyfuss, Robert (2006) *Devil's Game: How the United States Helped Unleash Fundamentalist Islam*, New York: Metropolitan.

Dudouet, Véronique (2013) 'Dynamics and Factors of Transition from Armed Struggle to Nonviolent Resistance', *Journal of Peace Research* 50(3): 401–413.

Eatwell, Roger (2006) 'Community Cohesion and Cumulative Extremism in Contemporary Britain', *The Political Quarterly* 77(2): 204–2016.

Ebner, Julia (2017) *The Rage: The Vicious Circle of Islamist and Far-Right Extremism*, London and New York: I.B. Tauris.

Edwards, Phil (2016) 'Closure through Resilience: The Case of Prevent', *Studies in Conflict and Terrorism* 39(4): 292–307.

Elden, Stuart (2007) 'There Is a Politics of Space Because Space Is Political: Henri Lefebvre and the Production of Space', *Radical Philosophy Review* 10(2): 101–16.

El-Said, Hamed and Harrigan, Jane (2012) *Deradicalising Violent Extremists: Counter-Radicalisation and Deradicalisation Programmes and Their Impact in Muslim Majority States*, London and New York: Routledge.

Enders, Walters and Sandler, Todd (2005) 'After 9/11: Is It All Different Now?' *Journal of Conflict Resolution* 49(2): 259–77, p. 260.

Espinoza, Marina (2018) 'State Terrorism: Orientalism and the Drone Programme', *Critical Studies on Terrorism* 11(2): 376–93.

Esposito, John L. and Iner, Derya (eds) (2019) *Islamophobia and Radicalization: Breeding Intolerance and Violence*, Basingstoke: Palgrave Macmillan.

Farrall, Stephan (2002) *Rethinking What Works with Offenders. Probation, Social Context and Desistance from Crime*, Devon: Willan.

Feierstein, Daniel (2014) *Genocide as Social Practice*, New York: Rutgers University Press.

Feldman, M. (2015) *From Radical-Right Islamophobia to 'Cumulative Extremism'*, London: Faith Matters.

Field, Anthony (2017) 'The Dynamics of Terrorism and Counterterrorism: Understanding the Domestic Security Dilemma', *Studies in Conflict & Terrorism* 40(6): 470–83.

Figueroa Ibarra, Carlos (2013) 'Genocide and State Terrorism in Guatemala, 1954–1996: An Interpretation', *Bulletin of Latin American Research* 32(s1): 151–73.

Fink, Naureen C and Hearne, Ellie B. (2008) *Beyond Terrorism: Deradicalization and Disengagement from Violent Extremism*, New York: International Peace Institute.

Foucault, Michel (1980) *Power/Knowledge: Selected Interviews and Other Writings 1972–1977*, New York: Pantheon.

Foucault, Michel (2004) *The Birth of Biopolitics*, Basingstoke: Palgrave Macmillan.

Furlow, R.B. and Goodall, H.L. (2011) 'The War of Ideas and the Battle of Narratives: A Comparison of Extremist Storytelling Structures', *Cultural Studies ↔ Critical Methodologies* 11(3): 215–23.

Gagnon Jr, VP (1994) 'Ethnic Nationalism and International Conflict: The Case of Serbia', *International Security* 19(3): 130–66.

Garrison, Arthur H. (2007) 'Defining Terrorism: Philosophy of the Bomb, Propaganda by Deed and Change through Fear and Violence', *Criminal Justice Studies* 17(4): 259–79.

Gaston, Sophie (2017) *Briefing Paper: Far-Right Extremism in the Populist Age*, London: Demos.

Giddens, Anthony (1991) *Modernity and Self-Identity: Self and Society in the Late Modern Age*, Stanford, CA: Stanford University Press.

Gielen, Amy-Jane (2018) 'Exit Programmes for Female Jihadists: A Proposal for Conducting Realistic Evaluation of the Dutch Approach', *International Sociology* 33(4): 454–72.

Global Research (2017) 'Non-Muslims Carried Out More Than 90% of All Terrorist Attacks in America', http://www.globalresearch.ca/non-muslims-carried-out-more-than-90-of-all-terrorist-attacks-in-america/5333619. Accessed 16 February 2017.

Goodwin, Matthew (2013) *The Roots of Extremism: The English Defence League and the Counter-Jihad Challenge*, London: Chatham House, p. 3.

Gurr, Ted R. (1970) *Why Men Rebel*, Princeton, NJ: Princeton University Press.

Hafez, Farid (2014) 'Shifting Borders: Islamophobia as Common Ground for Building Pan-European Right-Wing Unity', *Patterns of Prejudice* 48(5): 479–99.

Hasan, Md. Mahmudul (2017) 'The Rohingya Crisis: Suu Kyi's False Flag and Ethnic Cleansing in Arakan', *Irish Marxist Review* 6(19): 50–61.

Heath, Anthony and Demireva, Neli (2014) 'Has Multiculturalism Failed in Britain?', *Ethnic and Racial Studies* 37(1): 161–80.

Heath-Kelly, Charlotte (2017) 'The Geography of Pre-Criminal Space: Epidemiological of Radicalisation Risk in the UK Prevent Strategy, 2007–2017', *Critical Studies on Terrorism* 10(2): 297–319.

Hegghammer, Thomas (2010) 'The Rise of Muslim Foreign Fighters: Islam and the Globalization of Jihad', *International Security* 35(3): 53–94.

Hiebert, Maureen S. (2017) *Constructing Genocide and Mass Violence: Society, Crisis, Identity*, Abingdon: Routledge.

Hoffman, Bruce (1998) *Inside Terrorism*, New York: Columbia University Press.

Holbrook, Donald (2013) 'Far Right and Islamist Extremist Discourses: Shifting Patterns of Enmity', in M. Taylor, P.M. Currie, & D. Holbrook (eds) *Extreme Right Wing Political Violence and Terrorism*, New York: Bloomsbury Academic, pp. 215–37.

Horgan, John (2008) Deradicalization or Disengagement? A Process in Need of Clarity and a Counterterrorism Initiative in Need of Evaluation, *Perspectives on Terrorism* 2(4): 3–8.

Horgan, John (2009a) 'Individual Disengagement: A Psychological Analysis', in T. Bjørgo and J. Horgan (eds) *Leaving Terrorism Behind*, London and New York: Routledge, pp. 17–29.

Horgan, John (2009b) *Walking away from Terrorism: Accounts of Disengagement from Radical and Extremist Movements*, London and New York: Routledge.

Horgan, John (2014) *The Psychology of Terrorism*, London and New York: Routledge.

Horgan, John and Braddock, Kurt (2010) 'Rehabilitating the Terrorists?: Challenges in Assessing the Effectiveness of De-radicalization Programs', *Terrorism and Political Violence* 22(2): 267–91.

Hwang, Julie Chernov (2017) 'The Disengagement of Indonesian Jihadists: Understanding the Pathways', *Terrorism and Political Violence* 29(2): 277–95.

Institute for Economics and Peace (2019) *Global Terrorism Index 2019: Measuring the Impact of Terrorism*, Sydney: IEP.

Jäckle, Sebastian and Baumann, Marcel (2017) '"New Terrorism" = Higher Brutality? An Empirical Test of the "Brutalization Thesis"', *Terrorism and Political Violence* 29(5): 875–901, p. 875.

Jackson, Richard (2005) *Writing the War on Terrorism: Language, Politics and Counter-Terrorism*, Manchester: Manchester University Press.

Jackson, Richard (2008) 'The Ghosts of State Terror: Knowledge, Politics and Terrorism Studies', *Critical Studies on Terrorism* 1(3): 377–92.

Jackson, Richard, Smyth, Marie Breen and Gunning, Jeroen (eds) (2009) *Critical Terrorism Studies: A New Research Agenda*, London and New York: Routledge.

Jacobs, Janet (2017) 'The Memorial at Srebrenica: Gender and the Social Meanings of Collective Memory in Bosnia-Herzegovina', *Memory Studies* 10(4): 423–9.

Jarvis, Lee and Lister, Michael (2012) 'Disconnected Citizenship? The Impacts of Anti-Terrorism Policy on Citizenship in the UK', *Political Studies* 61(3): 656–75.

Jasko, Katarzyna Jasko, LaFree, Gary and Kruglansk, Arie (2016) 'Quest for Significance and Violent Extremism: The Case of Domestic Radicalization', *Political Psychology* 38(5): 815–31.

Johnson, Peter (2013) 'The Geographies of Heterotopia', *Geography Compass* 7(11): 790–803.

Jones, Adam (2006) *Genocide: A Comprehensive Introduction*, Abingdon: Routledge.

Jones, Seth and Libicki, Martin (2008) *How Terrorist Groups End. Lessons for Countering al Qa'ida*, Santa Monica, CA: RAND Corporation, pp. viii–xiv.

Jones, Seth G. (2018) *The Rise of Far-Right Extremism in the United States*, Washington, DC: Center for Strategic and International Studies Brief's (November).

Kallis, Aristotle, Zeiger, Sara and Öztürk, Bilgehan (eds) (2018) *Violent Radicalisation and Far-Right Extremism in Europe*, Ankara, Turkey: Foundation for Political, Economic and Social Research.

Kapitan, Tomis (2004) 'State Terrorism and Counter-Terrorism', in Igor Primoratz (ed.) *Terrorism: The Philosophical Issues*, Basingstoke: Palgrave Macmillan, pp. 175–91.

Kaplan, Jeffry, Lööw, Heléne and Malkki, Leena (2014) 'Introduction to the Special Issue on Lone Wolf and Autonomous Cell Terrorism', *Terrorism and Political Violence* 26(1): 1–12.

Khan, Waheeda and Majumdar, Sramana (2000) 'Qualitative Exploration of Salient Incidents of Violence Exposure among Youth in Kashmir: Beyond Direct Violence', in M. Seedat et al. (eds) *Enlarging the Scope of Peace*

Psychology, Springer International, Utrecht, NL: Peace Psychology Book Series, pp. 39–54.

Kimmel, Michael S. (2018) 'The Contemporary "Crisis" of Masculinity in Historical Perspective', in H. Brod (ed.) *The Making of Masculinities*, London: Routledge.

Knott, Kim, Lee, Benjamin and Copeland, Simon (2018) *Briefings: Reciprocal Radicalisation – Full Report*, Lancaster University: Centre for Research and Evidence on Security Threats.

Koehler, Daniel (2015) 'De-radicalisazation and Disengagement as Counter-Terrorism and Prevention Tools. Insights From Field Experiences Regarding German Right-Wing Extremism and Jihadism', M. Lombadri et al. (eds) *Countering Radicalisation and Violent Extremism among Youth to Prevent Terrorism*, Amsterdam: IOS, pp. 120–50.

Koehler, Daniel (2016) 'Right-Wing Extremism and Terrorism in Europe: Current Developments and Issues for the Future', *Prism: A Journal of the Center for Complex Operations* 4(2): 84–104.

Koehler, Daniel (2016) *Right-Wing Terrorism in the 21st Century: The 'National Socialist Underground' and the History of Terror from the Far-Right in Germany*, Abingdon: Routledge.

Kundnani, Arun (2014) *The Muslims Are Coming: Islamophobia, Extremism, and the Domestic War on Terror*, London and New York: Verso.

Lee, Martin A. (1999) *The Beast Reawakens: Fascism's Resurgence from Hitler's Spymasters to Today's Neo-Nazi Groups and Right-Wing Extremists*. London: Routledge.

Lewis, Hannah and Craig, Gary (2014) '"Multiculturalism Is Never Talked about": Community Cohesion and Local Policy Contradictions in England', *Policy and Politics* 42(1): 21–38.

Leydesdorff, Selma (2011) *Surviving the Bosnian Genocide: The Women of Srebrenica Speak*, Bloomington: Indiana University Press.

Lindekilde, Lasse (2012) 'Value for Money? Problems of Impact Assessment of Counter-Radicalization Policies on End Target Groups: The Case of Denmark', *European Journal on Criminal Policy and Research* 18: 385–402.

Lowe, David (2017) '"Prevent" Strategies: The Problems Associated in Defining Extremism – The Case of the UK', *Studies in Conflict and Terrorism* 40(11): 917–33.

Maher, Shiraz (2016) *Salafi-Jihadism: The History of an Idea*, London and New York: Hurst and Oxford University Press.

Malet, David (2013) *Foreign Fighters: Transnational Identity in Civil Conflicts*, New York: Oxford University Press.

Marsden, Sarah V. (2017) *Reintegrating Extremists: Deradicalisation and Desistance*, Basingstoke: Palgrave-Pivot.

Marsden, Sarah V. (2018) '"Deradicalisation" and Desistance: A Framework for Supporting the Reintegration of Extremists', *Lancaster University Centre for Research and Evidence on Security Threats Crest Security Review*, 7: 4–5.

Maslow, Abraham H. (1954) *Motivation and Personality*, New York: Harper and Row.

McCrisken, Trevor (2011) 'Ten Years on: Obama's War on Terrorism in Rhetoric and Practice', *International Affairs* 87(4): 781–801.

McDowell, Linda (2000) 'The Trouble with Men? Young People, Gender Transformations and the Crisis of Masculinity', *International Journal of Urban and Regional Research* 24(1): 201–9.

Meeteren, Masja and Oostendorp, Linda (2018) 'Are Muslims in the Netherlands Constructed as a "Suspect Community"? An Analysis of Dutch Political Discourse on Terrorism in 2004–2015', *Crime, Law and Social Change* 71(5): 525–40.

Melzer, Ralf and Serafin, Sebastian (2013) *Right-Wing Extremism in Europe*, Berlin: Friedrich-Ebert-Stiftung.

Moghaddam, Fathali M. (2005) 'The Staircase to Terrorism: A Psychological Exploration', *American Psychologist* 60(2): 161–9.

Muslim Council of Britain (2015) *British Muslims in Numbers: A Demographic, Socio-Economic and Health Profile of Muslims in Britain Drawing on the 2011 Census*, London: MCB.

NCTV (2018) *Fluctuating Waves of Right-Wing Extremist Violence in Western Europe*, The Hague: Ministry of Justice and Security.

Neumann, Peter (2008) 'Introduction', in P.R. Neumann (ed.) *Perspectives on Radicalisation and Political Violence – Papers from the First International Conference on Radicalisation and Political Violence*, London: Kings College International Centre for the Study of Radicalisation and Political Violence.

Neumann, Peter and Rogers, Brooke (2007) *Recruitment and Mobilisation for the Islamist Militant Movement in Europe*, London: Kings College International Centre for the Study of Radicalisation and Political Violence.

Norris, Pippa, Kern, Montague and Just, Marion (eds) (2003) *Framing Terrorism: The News Media, the Government and the Public*, London and New York: Routledge.

O'Donnell, Aislinn (2015) 'Securitisation, Counterterrorism and the Silencing of Dissent: The Educational Implications of "Prevent"', *British Journal of Educational Studies* 64(1): 53–76.

OHCHR (2017) *Guidance to States on Human Rights-Compliant Responses to the Threat Posed by Foreign Fighters*, New York: United Nations Office of the United Nations High Commissioner for Human Rights et al.

Özerdem, Alpaslan and Podder, Sukanya (2011) 'Disarming Youth Combatants: Mitigating Youth Radicalization and Violent Extremism', *Journal of Strategic Security* 4(4): 63–80.

Pantazis, Christina and Pemberton, Simon (2009) 'From the "Old" to the "New" Suspect Community: Examining the Impacts of Recent UK Counter-Terrorist Legislation', *British Journal of Criminology* 49(5): 646–66.

Papadopoulos, Linda (2010) *Sexualisation of Young People: Review*, London: Home Office.

Pappé, Ilan (2006) *The Ethnic Cleansing of Palestine*, Oxford: Oneworld.

Peach, Ceri (1994) 'The Meaning of Segregation', *Planning Practice and Research* 11(2): 137–50.

Pisoiu, Daniela (2015) 'Subcultural Theory Applied to Jihadi and Right-Wing Radicalization in Germany', *Terrorism and Political Violence* 27(1): 9–28.

Pisoiu, Daniela and Ahmed, Reem (2016) 'Capitalizing on Fear: The Rise of Right-Wing Populist Movements in Western Europe', in Institute for Peace Research and Security Policy at the University of Hamburg (ed.) *OSCE Yearbook 2015*, Baden-Baden: Germany, pp. 165–76.

Pratt, Douglas (2015) 'Islamophobia as Reactive Co-radicalization', *Islam and Christian–Muslim Relations* 26(2): 205–18.

Primoratz, Igor (2002) 'State Terrorism and Counter-Terrorism', in Igor Primoratz (ed.) *Terrorism: The Philosophical Issues*, Basingstoke: Palgrave Macmillan, pp. 113–27.

Qureshi, Asim (2015) '"PREVENT": Creating "Radicals" to Strengthen anti-Muslim Narratives', *Critical Studies on Terrorism* 8(1): 181–91.

Raffie, Dina Al (2013) 'Social Identity Theory for Investigating Islamic Extremism in the Diaspora', *Journal of Strategic Security* 6(4): 67–91.

Ragazzi, Francesco (2016) 'Suspect Community or Suspect Category? The Impact of Counterterrorism as "Policed Multiculturalism"', *Journal of Ethnic and Migration Studies* 42(5): 724–41.

Ragazzi, Francesco (2017) 'Countering Terrorism and Radicalisation: Securitising Social Policy?' *Critical Social Policy* 37(2): 163–79.

Rapoport, David C. (2004) 'The Four Waves of Modern Terrorism', in A.K. Cronin and J.M. Ludes (eds) *Attacking Terrorism: Elements of a Grand Strategy*, Washington, DC: Georgetown University Press, pp. 46–73.

Richardson, Louise and Weinberg, Leonard (2003) 'Conflict Theory and the Trajectory of Terrorist Campaigns in Western Europe', in A. Silke (ed.) *Research on Terrorism: Trends, Achievements and Failures*, London: Frank Cass, pp. 138–60.

Rogers, Paul (2013) 'Lost Cause: Consequences and Implications of the War on Terror', *Critical Studies on Terrorism* 6(1): 13–28.

Romaniuk, Peter (2015) *Does CVE Work? Lessons Learned from the Global Effort to Counter Violent Extremism*, Washington, DC: Global Center on Cooperative Security, September.

Rzepnikowska, Alina (2019) 'Racism and Xenophobia Experienced by Polish Migrants in the UK before and after Brexit Vote', *Journal of Ethnic and Migration Studies* 45(1): 61–77.

Sageman, Marc (2008) 'A Strategy for Fighting International Islamist Terrorists', *The ANNALS of the American Academy of Political and Social Science* 618(1): 223–31.

Sageman, Mark (2004) *Understanding Terror Network*. Philadelphia: University of Pennsylvania Press.

Saull, Richard (2015) 'Capitalism, Crisis and the Far-Right in the Neoliberal Era', *Journal of International Relations and Development* 18(1): 25–51.

Schmid, Alex P. (2010) 'Frameworks for Conceptualising Terrorism', *Terrorism and Political Violence* 16(2): 197–221.

Schmid, Alex P. (2013) *Radicalisation, De-radicalisation, Counter-Radicalisation: A Conceptual Discussion and Literature Review*, The Hague: The International Centre for Counter-Terrorism.

Schuurman, Bart and Bakker, Edwin (2016) 'Reintegrating Jihadist Extremists: Evaluating a Dutch Initiative, 2013–2014', *Behavioral Sciences of Terrorism and Political Aggression* 8(1): 66–85.

Schuurman, Bart and Eijkman, Quirine (2015) 'Indicators of Terrorist Intent and Capability: Tools for Threat Assessment', *Dynamics of Asymmetric Conflict* 8(3): 215–31.

Schuurman, Bart, Bakker, Edwin and Eijkman, Quirine (2016) 'Structural Influences on Involvement in European Homegrown Jihadism: A Case Study', *Terrorism and Political Violence* 30(1): 97–115.

Sedgwick, Mark (2010) 'The Concept of Radicalization as a Source of Confusion', *Terrorism and Political Violence* 22(4): 479–94.

Sekulić, Duško (2007) 'Ethnic Cleansing', in George Ritzer (ed.) *The Blackwell Encyclopedia of Sociology*, Oxford: Wiley, pp. 1450–2.

Simpson, Ludi (2004) 'Statistics of Racial Segregation: Measures, Evidence and Policy', *Urban Studies* 41(3): 661–81.

Spalek, B. (2016) 'Radicalisation, De-radicalisation and Counter-Radicalisation in Relation to Families: Key Challenges for Research, Policy and Practice', *Security Journal* 29(1): 39–52.

Sterkenburg, Nikki, Gssime, Yasmine and Meines, Marije (2019) *Local-Level Management of Far-Right Extremism*, Rotterdam: Radicalisation Awareness Network.

Stone, Dan (2004) 'The Historiography of Genocide: Beyond "Uniqueness" and Ethnic Competition', *Rethinking History* 8(1): 127–42.

Sumpter, Cameron (2017) 'Countering Violent Extremism in Indonesia: Priorities, Practice and the Role of Civil Society', *Journal of Deradicalisation* 11: 112–47.

Taylor, Charles (1994) *Multiculturalism and the Politics of Recognition*, Princeton, NJ: Princeton University Press.

TE-SAT (2018) *European Union Terrorist Situation and Trend Report*, The Hague: EUROPOL.

Ther, Philipp (2016) *The Dark Side of Nation-States: Ethnic Cleansing in Modern Europe*, New York and Oxford: Berghahn.

Thomas, Paul (2012) *Responding to the Threat of Violent Extremism: Failing to Prevent*, London: Bloomsbury.

Tucker, David (2001) 'What Is New about the New Terrorism and How Dangerous Is It?' *Terrorism and Political Violence* 13(3): 1–14.

Tucker, Robert C. (1967) 'The Deradicalization of Marxist Movements', *The American Political Science Review* 61(2): 343–58;

Uhlmann, Milena (2008) 'European Converts to Terrorism', *Middle East Quarterly* 15(3): 31–7.

United Nations (1948) *Convention on the Prevention and Punishment of the Crime of Genocide* (no. 1021).

United Nations General Assembly (2015) *Plan of Action to Prevent Violent Extremism*, New York: UNGA A/70/674.

United Nations Human Rights Council (2018) *Report of the Independent International Fact-Finding Mission on Myanmar* A/HRC/39/64, New York: UN.

US Agency for International Development (2011) *The Development Response to Violent Extremism and Insurgency: Putting Principles into Practice*, Washington, DC: USAID.

USAID (2009) *Guide to the Drivers of Violent Extremism*, Washington, DC: United States Agency for International Development, pp. 65–6.

Veldhuis, Tinka (2012) *Designing Rehabilitation and Reintegration Programmes for Violent Extremist Offenders: A Realist Approach*, The Hague: The International Centre for Counter-Terrorism.

Vellenga, Sipco and Groot Kees de (2019) 'Securitization, Islamic Chaplaincy, and the Issue of (De)radicalization of Muslim Detainees in Dutch Prisons', *Social Compass* 66(2): 224–37.

Venhaus, John (2010) *Why Youth Join Al-Qaeda*, Washington, DC: United States Institute of Peace.

Vidino, Lorenzo, Marone, Francesco and Entenmann, Eva (2017) *Fear Thy Neighbor: Radicalization and Jihadist Attacks in the West*. Leiden: George Washington University's Program on Extremism, The Hague: The Italian Institute for International Political Studies and the International Centre for Counter-Terrorism.

Wagner, Markus and Meyer, Thomas M. (2016) 'The Radical Right as Niche Parties? The Ideological Landscape of Party Systems in Western Europe, 1980–2014', *Political Studies* 65(1S): 84–107.

Webber, David and Kruglanski, Arie W. (2018) 'The Social Psychological Makings of a Terrorist', *Current Opinion in Psychology* 19: 131–4.

Weinstein, Jeremy M. (2005) 'Resources and the Information Problem in Rebel Recruitment', *Journal of Conflict Resolution* 49(4): 598–624.

Weitz, Eric D. (2015) *A Century of Genocide: Utopias of Race and Nation*, Princeton, NJ: Princeton University Press.

Wikström, Per-Olof H and Bouhana, Noémie (2017) 'Analyzing Radicalization and Terrorism: A Situational Action Theory', in G. LaFree and J.D. Freilich (eds) *The Handbook of the Criminology of Terrorism*, Oxford: Wiley Blackwell, pp. 175–86.

Wiktorowicz, Quinton (2005) *Radical Islam Rising: Muslim Extremism in the West*, London and New York: Rowman and Littlefield.

Wolfendale, Jessica (2007) 'Terrorism, Security, and the Threat of Counterterrorism', *Studies in Conflict and Terrorism* 30(1): 75–92.

Young, Jock (1999) *The Exclusive Society: Social Exclusion, Crime and Difference in Late Modernity*, London: Sage.

Younis, Tarek and Jadhav, Sushrut (2019) 'Islamophobia in the National Health Service: An Ethnography of Institutional Racism in PREVENT's Counter-Radicalisation Policy', *Sociology of Health & Illness* 42(3): 610–26.

Zarni, Maung and Cowley, Alice (2014) 'The Slow-Burning Genocide of Myanmar's Rohingya', *Pacific Rim Law and Policy Journal Association* 23(3): 683–754.

Zelin, Aaron Y. (2015) 'Picture or It Didn't Happen: A Snapshot of the Islamic State's Official Media Output', *Perspectives on Terrorism* 9(4): 85–97.

Index

Aarhus model 109, 124, 129
Afghanistan 11, 32–6, 58, 168–71
al-Baghdadi, Abu Bakr 156
Al-Muhajiroun 85
Al Qaeda 11, 12, 33–5, 68, 73
Al-Shabab 34
Alternative für Deutschland (AfD) 93
Arab Spring 34, 35
Arafat, Yasser 9, 10, 22, 145
Arakan Rohingya Salvation Army (ARSA) 49
Aum Shinrikyo 12, 162
Azad Kashmiris 26, 27, 45
Azzam, Abdullah 168, 170

behavioural change 136, 138
bin Laden, Osama 32–4, 36, 163, 164, 168–70
biopolitics 4, 37, 39, 87
Boko Haram 34
Bosnian Muslims 46–8
Bosnian Serb 46, 47
Breivik, Anders Behring 80, 93, 149, 153, 173
British National Party (BNP) 98
Bush, George W. 11, 36, 164, 165, 170
Byron, Lord 167

Canadian Intelligence Service 60
causality 138
Christchurch mosque shootings 80, 149, 150, 152
civic nationalism 43, 44
Civil Contingencies Committee (COBRA) 99
Clinton, Bill 34, 164
coercion 65, 71–2
Cold War 10, 79, 87

community 3, 6, 43, 72, 73, 78, 85, 89, 99, 124
 building 105, 108, 113
 global faith 116
 homogenized 56
CONTEST (CT strategy) 101, 108
Convention on the Prevention and Punishment of the Crime of Genocide 40–1
counter-jihad 81, 93, 98, 173
counterterrorism (CT) 4, 6, 14, 15, 18, 29, 39, 53–5, 89, 100, 101, 103, 107–9, 113–15, 119, 120, 159, 163, 164, 172
 Al Qaeda 33–5
 drone programmes 36–7
 Islamic State 156–9
 radicalization and (in)security 30–1
 'war on terror' 32–3
Croatia 46

dehumanization 13, 20, 75, 90, 102, 165
deindustrialization 82, 83, 86
deradicalization 3, 75, 94, 102, 107, 108, 110, 115, 119–25, 128, 133–5, 149, 159. *see also* radicalization
 disengagement process 141–4
 monitoring and evaluation 135–9
 politics 145–7
 terrorism and 139–41
desistance 119, 123–4, 129, 131, 133
Desistance and Disengagement Programme (DDP) 124
disengagement 113, 119, 122–7, 129–31, 133, 134, 139, 141–5
disillusionment 75, 129–31
diversity 86–8

domestic grievances 67
domino effect 143, 144
drone programmes 36–7
dwindling support 140

economic relations 82–4
EDL 98
education 113
Elsheikh, El Shafee 156, 157
ethnic cleansing 4, 37, 39, 42–9, 150, 152. *see also* genocide
ethnic nationalism 39, 40–4, 77, 79–81, 84, 150, 151, 173
European Counter-Jihad Movement (ECJM) 93
external grievances 67
extremism
    far-right 6, 80, 81, 84, 90, 93–5, 97–102, 106, 111, 149, 150, 152, 166, 172–3
    Islamist 6, 10, 77, 81, 90, 94–6, 100–2, 110, 172–3
    jihadi 17, 93
    right-wing 79, 80, 88, 96–8, 101, 129, 130

far-right extremism 6, 80, 81, 84, 90, 93–5, 97–102, 106, 111, 149, 150, 152, 166, 172–3
financial crisis of 2008 82–3
First World War 9, 40, 171
foreign fighters 3, 6, 64, 68, 109, 120, 166–71
French Revolution 8, 18
Front National 99–100

Generation Identity 98
genocide 4, 39, 49, 172
    hyper-ethnic nationalism 40–2
    Rohingya 48–9
    state terrorism 42–4
Germany 64, 96–8, 100, 109, 128, 153, 156

globalization 7, 44, 54, 82–6, 90, 96, 98, 106, 151, 169–70
Global North 29, 149, 150, 153, 165
Global South 65, 67, 71–2, 128
Global Terrorism Database 28
Guantanamo Bay 157, 164–5

Hamas 19, 23
Hayat model 128–9
Herzl, Theodor 20
heterotopia 76
Holocaust 40–2
Hussein, Saddam 11, 163

ideational approach 125–6
identity formation 86, 149, 170
identity politics 81, 84, 90–1, 174
India 24–7, 39, 43–6, 168
internet 19, 25, 42, 54, 64, 70, 88, 101, 172
intersectional conditionality 143
involuntary movement 129–30
Iraq 3, 6, 10, 11, 32, 34, 35, 58, 64, 145, 157, 161, 163, 171
Islamic State 3, 6, 34, 35, 55, 57, 62, 64, 70, 71, 73, 75, 85, 96, 105, 107, 109, 111, 112, 119, 120, 127, 134, 145, 156–9, 161, 171
Islamism 5, 6, 19, 33, 72, 78, 81, 107, 157, 170
    anti-Islam 93, 100, 153, 173
Islamist extremism 6, 10, 77, 81, 90, 94–6, 100–2, 110, 172–3
Islamofascism 169–71
Islamophobia 6, 54, 75, 80, 100, 103, 105, 106, 109, 112, 115, 150, 152, 153, 157–9, 164
    and radicalization 153–6
Islam4UK 85
Israel 9, 10, 12, 20–3, 33, 39, 42, 98

Jammu and Kashmir 24, 26, 45. *see also* Kashmir
Jammu Kashmir Liberation Front 168

jihadi extremism 17, 93
Johnson, Boris 5, 158

Kashmir 4, 17, 18, 24–9, 44–6, 49, 168
Khan, Imran 26
Kotey, Alexanda 156, 157

Lefebvre, Henry 76
Lemkin, Raphael 40
le Pen, Marie 93
London bombings. *see* 7/7 London bombings

Madrid train bombings 34
masculinity 5, 83–6, 95, 106, 155
material
    benefits 70–2
    support 126
media 5, 7, 14, 25, 29, 59, 83, 99–102, 109, 111, 114, 151, 152, 154, 158, 165
    and politics 59, 83, 99–100, 109, 154, 158, 163
Middle East 11, 20, 23, 32–5, 59, 73, 113, 134, 152, 161–3, 166, 168, 171
migration 64, 77, 107, 111, 154
Milošević, Slobodan 47
Mladić, Ratko 47
mobilization 59–60, 87, 108, 162
    socialization in 61–5
multi-agency approach 128
multiculturalism 80, 84, 86, 87, 98, 99, 103, 107, 109, 110, 113, 151, 173
multi-pronged approach 126
Munich attack 12, 22, 162
Muslimness 109, 155, 156
Muslims 4–6, 17, 24–6, 29, 32, 33, 36, 39, 43, 55, 62, 64, 65, 67, 70, 73–5, 77–89, 93, 96, 98–103, 105–16, 150–9, 161, 164–6, 168–71, 173

anti-Muslim 6, 48, 80, 81, 93, 100, 112, 152, 153, 157, 168
Bosnian 46–8
British 105–10, 112, 114, 115, 153–5, 157, 158
    and Islam 98, 116
Kashmiri 44–6
Myanmar 48–9
Ummah 78, 169
Yugoslavia 46–8
Myanmar 4, 39, 48–9

nationalism 5, 26, 39–44, 46, 49, 77–81, 84, 149–51
neoliberalism 82, 84, 87
new alternatives 140
New American Century 34, 164
9/11 3, 11, 23, 27, 29, 32, 33, 37, 54, 81, 84, 88, 105, 116, 151, 162–4, 170
non-violence 139, 144, 145
Northern Ireland 25, 39, 134, 139, 141, 143, 146, 162

Obama, Barack 15, 36, 164, 165
ontological security 69
organizational breakdown 140
orientalism 36, 80, 150
'othering' process 47, 86, 90, 96, 100
Ottomans 152–3, 167

Pakistan 11, 24–7, 32, 33, 36, 44–6, 64, 128
Palestine 4, 18, 20–3, 25, 29, 143, 144, 146, 162, 171
Palestinian Liberation Organization (PLO) 9–10, 22, 23
Party for Freedom 99–100
pastoral techniques 126
personal grievances 5, 68–70
policymaking 17, 49, 78, 158
political movement 19, 143
political violence 7, 19, 29–31, 39,

43, 49, 56–9, 65, 72–3, 90, 110, 141, 144, 145, 152, 154–6, 161
politics
  biopolitics 4, 37, 39, 87
  from deradicalization 145–7
  identity 81, 84, 90–1, 174
  media and 59, 83, 99–100, 109, 154, 158, 163
  of terror 163–6
  Western European 97–9
populism 79, 80, 149, 151, 168
post-industrialization 82–4, 86, 151, 174
pre-criminal space 120
preliminary success 140
Prevent Duty 106
'Prevent' policy 105, 157
  challenges 105–7
  extent and limit 107–9
  far-right groups 114
  Islamophobia 115–16
  stigmatization 109–12
primitives 150
Pro Cologne 98
pro-integration 110, 124
psychological rehabilitation 126
push–pull factors 55–6, 77, 130–2

race war 153
radicalization 3–6, 15, 34, 39, 49, 53–6, 58–63, 67, 70, 73–7, 81–5, 88–91, 106–12, 114, 115, 119, 120, 122, 134–7, 149, 151–2, 158, 159, 165, 172–4
  convert 85
  and extremism 94–5
  Islamophobia and 153–6
  reciprocal (*see* reciprocal radicalization)
  and (in)security 30–1
rape 47–9, 153
Rashtriya Swayamsevak Sangh (RSS) 26
reciprocal radicalization 79–81, 93–7, 101–3

diversity 86–8
economic relations 82–4
far-right extremism 90, 93–5, 97–102
Islamist extremism 94, 95, 100–2
masculinity 84–6
media and politics 99–100
right-wing extremism 96–8, 101
war on terror 88–91
recognition 70, 86, 101, 146
recruitment 4, 6, 57–64, 111–13, 120, 162, 167
rehabilitation 113, 119
reign of terror 8
reintegration 119, 123–6, 134
right-wing extremism 79, 80, 88, 96–8, 101, 129, 130
Rohingya 39, 48–9

Salafi-jihadism 72–4
Salafism 5, 73
sanctioning 126
Saudi Arabia 33, 34, 128, 143, 168–70
Schmid, Alex P. 13
Second World War 9, 18, 21, 25, 42, 44, 82
self-actualization 70, 84, 87
self-selection 63–4
Serb media 47
7/7 London bombings 34, 53–5, 108, 116
sexual violence 47–8
Slovenia 46, 153
social
  alienation 68, 169
  approach 126
  media 48, 70, 111, 173
  mobility 5, 46, 82, 83, 87, 90, 111, 151, 155, 174
  movement 142, 143
  psychology 5, 74–6
  selection 63–4
  structure 90–1, 134
socialization 59, 61–5, 101, 149
space and place 76–8

Spain 43, 64, 97
spatial conditionality 143
Srebrenica 46–7
state terrorism 17, 29
   genocides 42–4
   history 17–20
   Kashmir, struggles in 24–8
   Palestine 20–3
state violence 14, 18, 39, 49, 143
Stern Gang 11–12
stigmatization 109–12, 116
strategic terrorism 21–3
strength-based approach 124
structural terrorism 21, 22
success 140
Sudan 33, 57
suicide bombing 15, 23, 27, 28, 162
Surviving the Genocide (2011) 48
Syria 3, 6, 10, 23, 35, 58, 143, 153, 156, 157, 161, 171

tailor-made approach 5, 127–8
Taliban 33, 34, 169
Tarrant, Brenton 149, 173
temporal conditionality 143
terrorist 11–15
theory of change 137
transnationalism 6, 154, 169–70
Trump, Donald 5, 37, 156, 157

ultra-violence 150
Ummah 78, 169
United States 5, 19, 32–4, 56, 83, 123, 149, 163, 166, 170, 171
UN Security Council 47

value expectancies 71
value expectations 71
violence 5, 7–9, 12, 21, 23, 31, 55, 73, 75, 88, 93, 95, 98, 103, 124, 133, 134, 143
   political 7, 19, 29–31, 39, 43, 49, 56–9, 65, 72, 90, 110, 141, 144, 145, 152, 154–6, 161
   sexual 47–8
   state 14, 18, 39, 49, 143
violent extremism (VE) 4, 6, 8, 16, 30, 53–64, 67, 68, 70, 71, 73, 76, 79, 87–9, 91, 105–12, 114, 116, 119, 120, 122, 128, 129, 137, 166, 173
vocational rehabilitation 126
voluntary movement 129–30
vulnerability 59, 61–3

war on terror 3–5, 11, 23, 29, 31–7, 39, 79, 86, 88–91, 100, 107, 112, 158, 164, 169
Western European politics and society 97–9
white nation 151–3
Wilders, Geert 93

Yugoslavia 4, 42, 43, 46–8

Zia Ul Haq, Muhammad 33
Zionism 20, 21

www.ingramcontent.com/pod-product-compliance
Ingram Content Group UK Ltd.
Pitfield, Milton Keynes, MK11 3LW, UK
UKHW030122030325
455743UK00008B/200